The Way It Used To Be
Stories from a Northern Town

Diane Solie Smith

Bradford D. Smith
Editor

Fathom Publishing Company
Anchorage, Alaska

ISBN 978-1-954896-68-0 Hardbound
ISBN 978-1-954896-67-3 Paperback
ISBN 978-1-954896-69-7 E-book

Library of Congress Control Number 2024914747
Printed in United States of America

Cover photo
   Brittani and Sabrina Holt.
Area maps
   Jacques Polomé, Jacques Polomé Design, Perth, Australia

bradfordsmithauthor.com

fathompublishing.com
Fathom Publishing Company
P.O. Box 200448
Anchorage, Alaska 99520-0448

Dedication

The pioneers, past and present,
who make Atlin
the greatest little town in the north.

Table of Contents

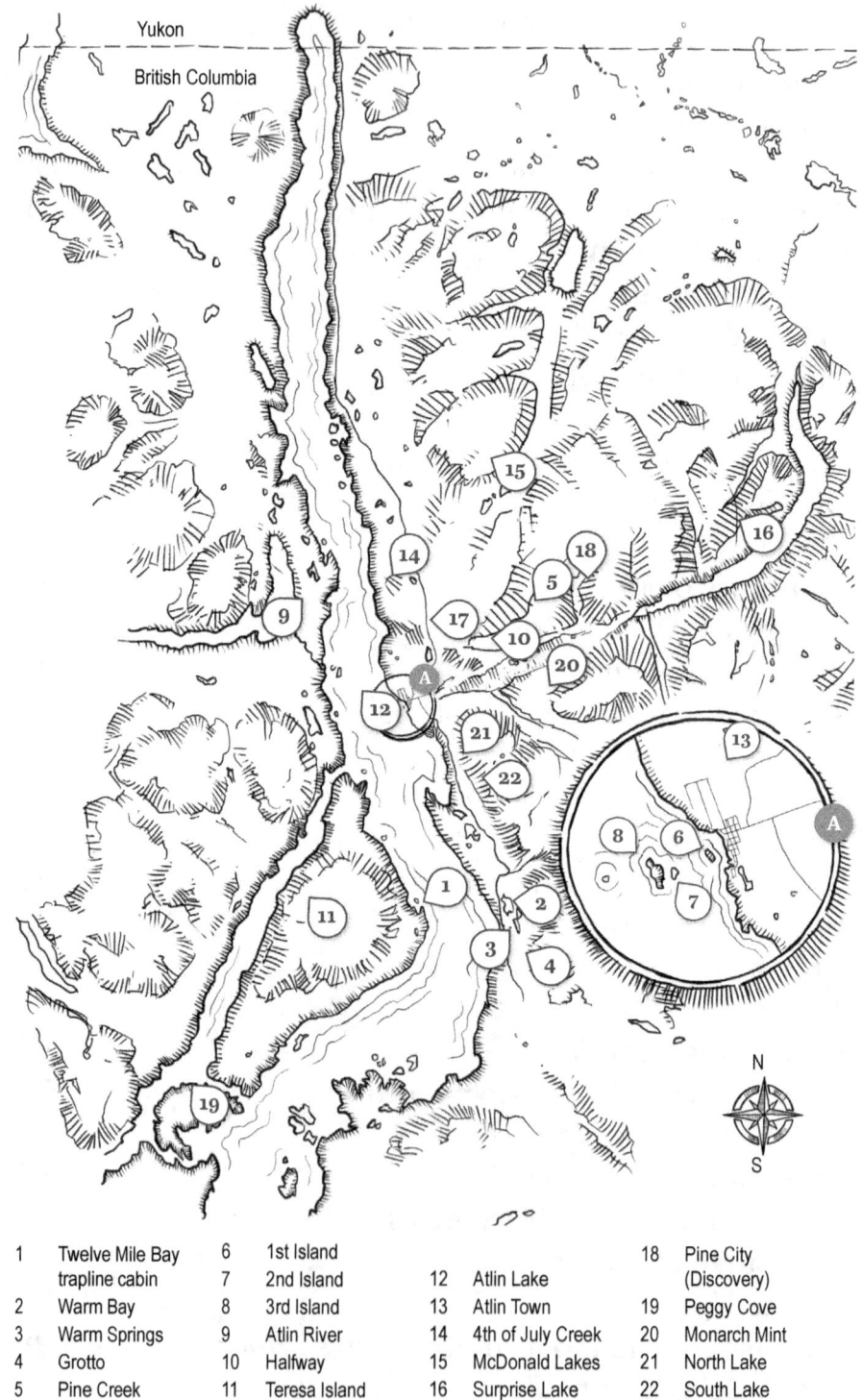

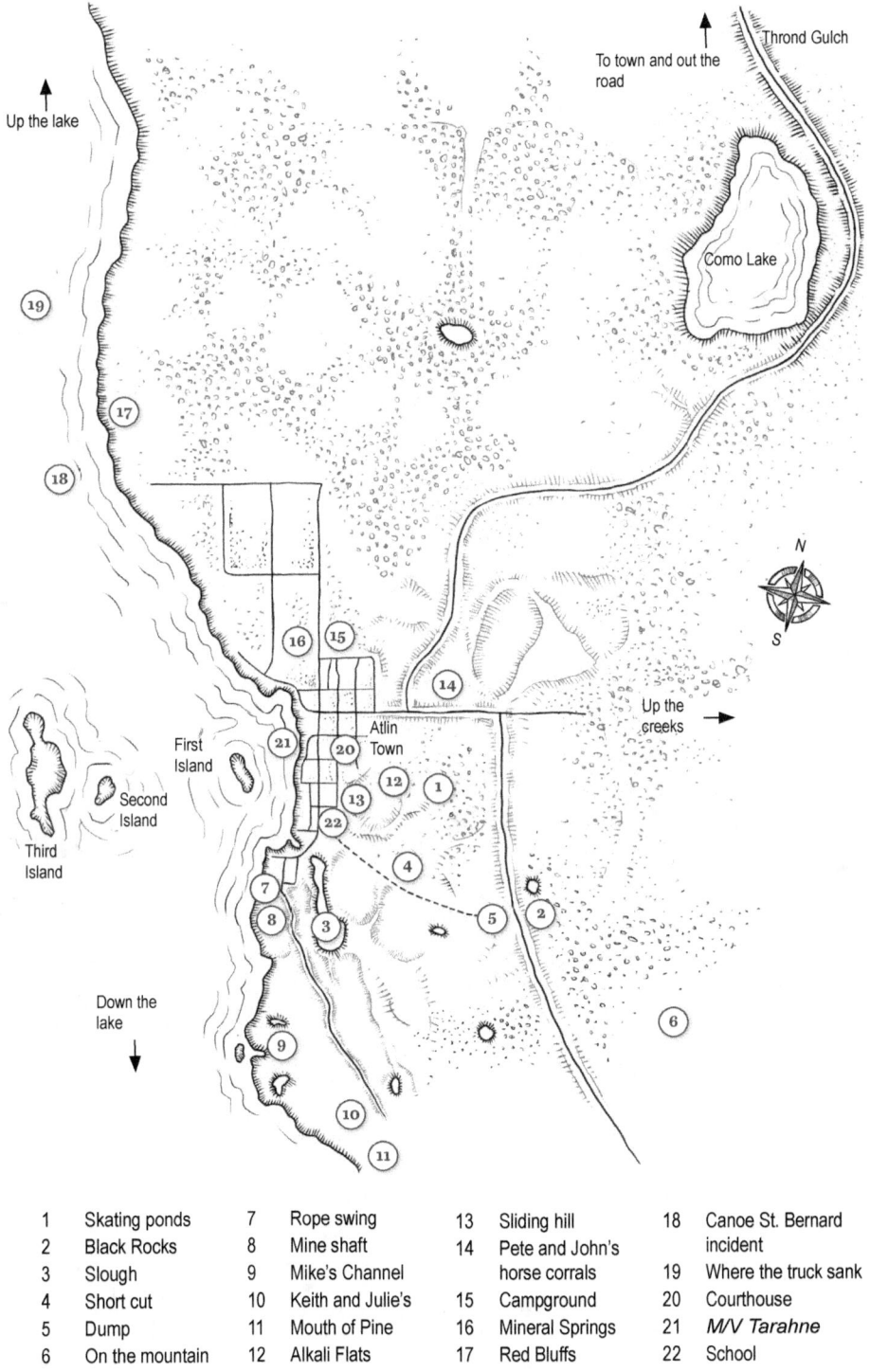

Up the lake

Throud Gulch

To town and out the
road

Como Lake

N

S

Up the
creeks

19

17

18

16 15

14

First
Island

21 20 Atlin
Town

Second
Island

13 12 1

22

Third
Island

4

7

5 2

8 3

Down the
lake

9

6

10

11

1	Skating ponds	7	Rope swing	13	Sliding hill	18	Canoe St. Bernard
2	Black Rocks	8	Mine shaft	14	Pete and John's		incident
3	Slough	9	Mike's Channel		horse corrals	19	Where the truck sank
4	Short cut	10	Keith and Julie's	15	Campground	20	Courthouse
5	Dump	11	Mouth of Pine	16	Mineral Springs	21	*M/V Tarahne*
6	On the mountain	12	Alkali Flats	17	Red Bluffs	22	School

vii

Editor's Note

The stories contained in this publication were written for the *Atlin News Miner* newspaper in Atlin, British Columbia, during the years 1972 to 1978 by Diane Solie Smith.

The collection was prepared and organized by Diane's son, Bradford Davis Smith, for reprint in *The Way It Used To Be: Stories From a Northern Town*.

Diane created the original advertisements that appeared in the *Atlin News Miner* for the Kootenay Hotel and the Discovery Shop that are included in this book.

The excerpts under the images at the start of each chapter are quotes from Diane's personal letters written to friends and family from 1967 to 1976.

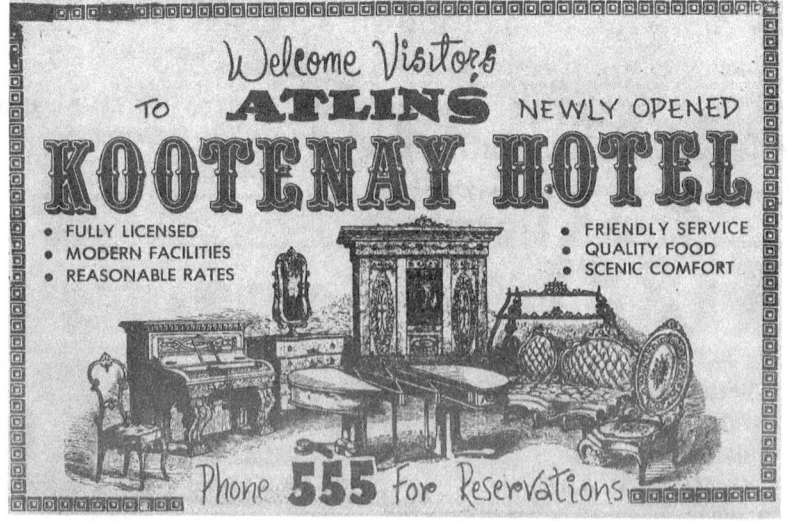

The Smiths are a solid part of Atlin. Diane tells her story . . .

Introduction

We came to Atlin in July of 1967 looking for something different. Found it, too! We escaped the old office doldrums but often find those mere eight-hour days have stretched to 12 or 14 or more. But it will never be considered a grind.

Shortly after moving here, Ed and I bought the old Kootenay Hotel. We had a rollicking summer in the hotel business followed soon after by a fire that leveled this old Koot. The next summer, with time in excess, I opened the

Discovery Shop. It was called The Bottle Shoppe then because that is about all it contained—old bottles. It was in the judge's chamber of the Old Government Building which we called home.

Years before, I had majored in commercial art at university. Then to avoid becoming another starving artist, I switched to engineering and finally put in 16 years as a draftsman [for the US Navy and the Coast Guard]. I learned a lot about plans and forgot a lot about art. But the yen to putter around with crafts never completely disappeared and the Discovery Shop was a reason to try some ideas.

That first fling at shop business made one thing clear. Atlin visitors needed a place to browse and ask questions. Most people weren't interested in old bottles, but they were interested in Atlin.

By the next year, we had put together a rather rustic museum in the old court room adjacent to the shop. The museum brought a lot of visitors and I soon found myself spending as much time guiding tours through the relics as tending the shop which by this time contained a number of hand-made items.

Eventually, our hope of turning over the museum to the town was realized when a Historical Society was formed under the deft guidance of Shirley Connolly. It was with an audible sigh of relief we relinquished the now greatly-expanded collection of relics to the Society.

The Discovery Shop quickly grew in volume of contents if not in physical size as more new artists and craftsmen sought outlets for their work. Customers were pleasantly surprised and obviously pleased to find gifts and souvenirs made right here in Atlin.

In 1974, the shop was relocated to the old Walter Sweet cabin at Third and Discovery Streets and briefly we enjoyed the luxury of additional space. This didn't last long. The workshop across the road produced more items and more craftsmen needed selling points.

The Discovery Workshop is specializing in jewelry of jade and gold nuggets, leather ware featuring moose hide shirts and jackets and small gift items. New work includes mitts and hats made of local furs and fur parkas. Probably there will be a Discovery Shop catalogue in print later this year and when that happens, the shop will really be a full-time, year-around job.

Atlin, British Columbia

In 1898, two Alaskan prospectors found gold on Pine Creek near Atlin Lake in British Columbia, Canada. Situated in the far northwest corner of the province, Atlin is roughly a hundred miles from Skagway, Alaska and thirty miles south of the Yukon border. The opening of the White Pass & Yukon Railway made Atlin only a two-day journey from Juneau, Alaska. Within months, the area was flooded with an estimated ten thousand prospectors, miners, and merchants.

At first, the town that sprung up on the shore of the vast lake consisted of a meager scattering of wall tents and false fronts. In only a matter of months with the addition of multiple hotels, eating establishments, food and sundry stores, and of course, bars, the town soon shed its image of gold-camp vulgarity and replaced it with an aura of sophistication and commitment to community.

Several town fires tested the resolve of the business owners and residents, but each time they rebuilt bigger and better. Gold continued to be plentiful and tourism was added to the prosperous economy by the White Pass & Yukon Railway Company. During the early 1900s, the town settled into a comfortable routine.

During the great depression and after the signing of the Gold Reserve Act in the United States which effectively banned personal ownership of gold, Atlin's economy slowed greatly. When World War II came along, the town withered. The men went off to war, tourism completely ceased, and the mining stopped. Families moved away and businesses were shuttered for good.

Although mining continued on a small scale throughout the decades and tourists trickled back in after the road was completed in 1956, there were few facilities to accommodate them.

Atlin walked a thin line for its very survival throughout the 1950s and into the early 1960s. For years, the town teetered between relevance and ghost town status. But at its very core, there were families that refused to let Atlin become a footnote in a gold rush history book. These were the families who built the town and over the years had insisted on its continued existence. These families were Atlin's backbone, its guts, its heart, and its essence. And they were patiently waiting for the next boom.

They didn't have long to wait. By the late 1960s, Atlin was becoming attractive to a variety of people. Americans came to start over and to escape the turmoil of their own country and the war in South East Asia. Canadians came looking for a safe and inclusive place to raise a family. Adventurers came to try living off the land. Artist and craftsman, inspired by the beauty and bounty, came to stay. For all these reasons, Atlin was experiencing a rebirth, a new gold rush so to speak.

By the mid-1970s, Atlin's population had doubled reaching approximately 250 people. Much like in its early years, businesses were opening up all over town. Another grocery store was added and they installed a gas pump giving the town a choice of two stations. The long-dormant hardware store was given new life by new owners who added more clothing and kitchen wares as well as hardware.

Gold prices were rising and prospecting and mining picked up. People were driving the Alaska Highway and more and more made their way down the road to Atlin.

A new hotel and small motel were being built, gift shops, and art galleries popped up, A fine community hall was built and new services were added every year. Atlin had its first newspaper in thirty years. This is the time when the stories presented here were written.

We are always amused when someone writes and asks us where on earth Atlin is. We are hidden away in the wilderness, the most northern town in British Columbia, Canada. We are just thirty miles from the Yukon border in the western part of the province. Atlin always has the misfortune of being hidden under the inserts for Vancouver and Victoria on maps so often we feel left out of British Columbia. Since most of our business is done in Whitehorse, Yukon Territory, we would be better off if we were a Yukon town.

Atlin: Many Things to Many People

Atlin is a youngster in the eyes of history. A scant seventy-two years old, it was founded when a prospector's pan first held tiny particles of Pine Creek gold, and men swarmed to grab a share of the wealth. Atlin boomed when the horse was king in the world of transportation, and when muscle, sweat, and curses were the major forces behind earth rending and operations that gouged gold from the streams. Atlin enjoyed a boisterous youth then settled into a declining middle age.

Atlin has always been many things to many people. Most of the first stampeders saw it only as a place to make a fast buck—a place to grab for the brass ring before

1

drifting on to the next strike. But many of the early gold seekers found it suited them as a place to settle down. For them, it was right for building homes, raising families, and becoming established in the community way of life. These were Atlin's real founding fathers. An unfortunate few found it a point of no return—a place of shattered dreams and lost hope. Others fell victim to a northern nature's fatal sword. For some, Atlin has been the end of the road, but for many, it has been the end of the rainbow.

The ones who stuck it out through the lean years are the ones to whom the later-day pioneers owe tribute. They were the stubborn ones who kept Atlin on the map when an economy based on gold production sagged disastrously and it was often a challenge to keep body and soul together. A unique combination of the "Atlin Spell" and the tough perseverance of these settlers kept the town quietly alive while another place would have faded into history.

Atlin waited while the world outside passed through decades of war and prosperity, then into a time of restlessness born of overcrowding and a singular dedication to materialistic pursuits. Atlin became a little quieter and emptier while clinging to the hope another boom would occur but unaware it would be quite different from the first.

The village has a charm, now rare. An old-fashioned atmosphere prevails that is balm to a victim of the plastic and chrome world to the south. Here the new log buildings blend amiably with the old false fronts. The sound of horse bells and the clop, clop of hooves is heard in the streets. A malamute's wail may rent the still night and whirring chopper blades may cut crystal clear air, but the sense-dulling din of factory and traffic do not exist.

Atlin offers solace to the harried spirit worn ragged by the push-pull of the city. It offers vast miles of surrounding wilderness for the sportsman, the nature lover, or loner who simply wants room in which to think.

Atlin lacks many amenities, but the inconvenience of outhouses and water-storage barrels is offset by an easygoing air. Time is available to exchange a yarn over a cup of tea or to listen to the tinkle of the ice along the lakeshore. Time is also available to skin a moose or to help a neighbor start a frozen truck. Time is, very likely, part of Atlin's newly found wealth, discovered and highly prized by the new pioneers who harbor vivid memories of the mad-hatter pace of other places.

Atlin is also a place in which to change the course of a life. People come here searching for new surroundings, new friends, and new adventures. The town draws those who have jogged themselves from old worn ruts and are now experiencing the joys and pitfalls of trying something entirely different.

Here an electronics technician operates a grocery store, an iron worker owns a new hotel, a man who worked in broadcast sales and public relations at a Toronto radio station has a small motel and has just begun gold mining, while his wife, a former media director with an ad agency, prepares to open an art gallery. A registered nurse, a telephone operator, and a draftsman have gift and craft stores. A young couple with degrees in psychology and education have opened a general store. A former die cutter has been a cook at a hunting camp, fought a forest fire, dug graves, worked at construction, and is currently driving a truck at the highway department—a mixed bag, to be sure, but in all cases certainly a change. For a few city-bred young people, Atlin has been a place to try a Tom Sawyer type of existence denied them in an urban childhood. It is a place for them to experience life in the bush and to try a little living off the land. Some newcomers are doing things long dreamed of—like running a trapline, driving a dog team, working a placer claim, building a log house.

As in the early days, many people of many skills, professions, and talents are gathering here and blending into the community. Each add to the continuity and continuing life of a busy, rejuvenated Atlin. And each find that Atlin has a special meaning for them.

Today we had a frigid north wind blowing down the lake. The temperature is twenty-five below and the lake is "steaming" as it does when it is below zero and it hasn't frozen. It is a good day to sit inside in the cozy warmth and let the icicles form out there. During this time before freeze up, we sit under a cloud. The whole lake area is enshrouded in mist and to see blue sky and sunshine, we have to go a couple miles out of town and away from the lake. It is interesting to see from a distance because when all else is bright and blue, a ninety-mile-long trail of mist hangs in the lake valley. As soon as ice forms over the whole lake, the mist is gone and we can enjoy the sun again. I hope freeze up comes before Christmas as it did last year.

Ghosts of Christmas Concerts Past

I remember our first Atlin Christmas concert. We joined the crowd at the aging Moose Hall that somehow looked beautifully festive that night. A sparkling tree stood near a shaky portable stage and loud whispers and titters came from behind homemade curtains. Mary Reid was the principal then and she and another girl attended twenty-nine students at a very old Atlin Elementary School. It was 1967.

A fate which often falls to the man of a new family had befallen my husband that particular year. He was given the dubious honor of playing Santa Claus. His stage career was nil and his temperature was three degrees over normal. He was positive he had the flu, but it was probably opening night jitters.

During his performance, a persistent little blonde kid kept tugging at his trouser leg while Santa muttered tersely "Beat it!" "Scram!" and tried to shake loose. Finally, the little kid said "Daddy!" in a loud and insistent voice and Santa's identity was known to all.

I can't remember much about the program that night but I do recall wondering how those teachers managed all the excited kids in the tiny room backstage.

After the program, the ladies of the Community Club served cookies and sandwiches and tea and coffee flowed like Pine Creek. The big Yukon wood stove crackled so efficiently everyone nearly roasted. Somehow this small discomfort was forgotten in lieu of the shining eyes of the smallest children as they received presents and candy from Santa-Daddy.

How different that magical night from the last Christmas program I attended when my older boy was a tiny blue spot on a distant stage in a huge new auditorium. Hollywood lighting effects accompanied a nearly professional production. No cookies or coffee followed the program— only a tense drive home through crowded wet streets.

The next two years, while Bob Greenhil was principal, the Christmas concert was held in the brand-new Atlin Elementary School. [Two double-wide trailers back-to-back.] I remember Greg and Kevin Neufeld singing together at one of the concerts—Kevin the picture of sober concentration while Greg grinned toothlessly from ear to ear. The next year when Betty Thoma was co-teacher and producer with Bob, Greg Kirkwood, and Mels Melberg cracked us up with a dazzling bit of stomach-muscle virtuosity done to the tune of 'Alley Cat.'

In 1970 and 1971, a live-wire Australian couple, Wayne

and Sandy Barwick, were our teachers. The town had grown and so had the school enrollment, so the concert was held again at the old Moose Hall. Wayne had taught the kids some flashy tumbling routines that were a grand finale to his first concert. John Harvey was new here, so he played Santa. He discovered a full black beard is quite a hindrance in the role of the famous white-haired elf.

The Christmas concert of 1971 was laced with certain nostalgia. We knew it would be the last time the old Moose Hall would resound with the sound of familiar carols and ring with the high excitement of a Christmas concert. The curling club had just received a government grant to build a new Recreation Centre. The old Moose Hall, which started life in Discovery during the gold rush as the Arctic Brotherhood Hall, would no longer be used for this all-important event.

At that last Moose Hall concert, a mixture of Australian and Northern humor turned "Tie Me Kangaroo Down, Boys" into "Tie Me Moose to a Spruce, Bruce." Sterling performances were abundant, but one I remember best was the lament of a "forty or so year-old waitress" for the loss of her logger sweetheart. The lesson learned was that loggers and gentlemen were synonymous and you can easily spot a logger because he "stirs his coffee with his thumb." The poignant accompaniment to this act was a harmonica solo recorded by Harold Colwell.

Later, when the older children recited the haunting lines from Robert Service's "The Spell of the Yukon," a tear slid down the wrinkled cheek of an old miner in the audience as memories of a lifetime in the north flooded back.

The curtains closed on a page in Atlin's history that night. After traditional coffee and cookies and presents were given by Santa Clive Aspinall [new in town], who betrayed his own identity with his English accent, nearly 200 people left the last Christmas Concert in the old Moose Hall.

Our eight-year-old son, Brad, entered the parade competition done up as an outhouse. It's a rather appropriate costume for a town with no sewer or water system. We spent two days and a couple of nights building his "building" out of an old refrigerator box. I painted it up and on the back made a sign, "Little Toot." He won the blue ribbon for being the best non-mechanized entry in the parade. He was quite proud of this. Oh yes, he carried a big bag of peanuts along and wherever he stopped, he would leave a pile.

Average Kid Atlin Variety

Here he comes down the middle of Second Avenue munching a chocolate bar just purchased at Mr. Craft's little candy and tobacco counter. He wears faded jeans with one ripped knee and a denim jacket with sleeves too short. He hazards a kick at a rock even though his toe sticks out of a hole in his runner. He has an Atlin home haircut easily identified by the rick-rack edge at the back and the molting chicken affect over each ear—the end result of a shearing by Mom who has yet to master the art of barbering. In his pocket, along with a tangled rabbit snare, are two very gray lumps of sugar, necessary supplies in case he should meet a friendly horse with a sweet tooth. Behind follows a large dog of dubious origin traveling a zig-zag course that takes him to all the best-smelling places.

This is the Average Atlin Kid and Company going about a day's business. Because females of all ages are outnumbered in Atlin, just as in the early days, Atlin's Average Kid is a boy. He is about nine years old. His way of life differs considerably from that of his counterparts in the southern reaches of British Columbia. There are a multitude of things he doesn't know about the modern world outside, but he has a special background of knowledge and experiences, perhaps more boys his age should have.

For Average Atlin Kid, a big city is Whitehorse, Yukon. Beyond his scope are places like Vancouver and Montreal. A shopping trip to Whitehorse may mean a chance to snatch a few minutes before the televisions in the department store while mom shops for a new blouse. A rare treat is an overnight trip to town and a whole evening of television in a motel with a real modern bathroom and endless gallons of hot water in which to shower.

He won't be able to tell you much about TV and can't discuss the latest hair- and eyebrow-raising movies. The old family entertainment flicks of the 1950s and early 1960s are what he sees at the Atlin Community Hall. But he could tell you a host of things that concern him more as a boy whose life is closely related to all things outdoors. He could take you along a snowy winter trail and identify each animal track that crossed your path. He could show you how to build a cubby for a lynx set. He could tell you what each hide is in a Hudson Bay fur room. He could probably tell you whether or not it was prime. He could identify most mineral-bearing-ore samples from around Atlin because he was a pretty good amateur geologist. He could show you how to pan for gold and how to operate a rocker box.

Average Atlin Kid has never seen a live snake or a skunk but he has watched a band of caribou cross the frozen lake in front of town. He has seen moose by the dozens along the roads he travels and has watched a skittish lynx sprint past the headlights of his dad's pickup across the trail in front of the dog team. He has never heard the exciting music and raucous barking of a circus or carnival and he couldn't identify the sounds of a busy city street. But he has listened to the thunder of the lake ice when pressure cracks form and he knows the faraway howl of a wolf.

Fresh watermelon, strawberries, and cherries are infrequent treats for Atlin's Average Kid. Things like artichokes, avocados, and eggplant are unknowns. But he suffers not at all from their absence in his diet. He is a sturdy, robust specimen whose winter diet centers on lean, delicious moose and caribou with grouse and lake trout for variety. His mother bakes the family bread and the mouth-watering aroma of fresh buns and cinnamon rolls often greets him at the end of the school day. He helps pick wild raspberries for shortcakes and jams and moss berries for pies and cobblers. There are black currant berries for burgundy-wine flavored jelly. Saskatoon berries, rose hips, wild cranberries, and gooseberries are made into syrups, sauces, and ketchups to whet the appetite of any growing boy.

His life is simple, uncluttered with pressures and

problems. He doesn't lack for excitement. It comes in unexpected forms—a forest fire near town, a moose hunt with dad, a surprise ride in a bush plane. The confidence with which he goes about the tasks of trapping, handling a horse, or chopping wood for the kitchen stove often belies his age. He is happy and outgoing, at ease with adults. He is normally full of fun and pranks but causes no serious trouble around town. He is at home in this corner of the northern wilderness; and one who is missing very little that is important to a well-rounded existence.

We moved here from Juneau, Alaska, four years ago. We are Americans by birth but northerners by choice. Up here it matters little which country you are in. The northern atmosphere and way of life spreads across Alaska and sub-arctic Canada. Our aim was to get away from those dreary years of trudging off to the office every day. We wanted to do something different before we really got in a rut and began thinking we were too old to make the break. I must say our experiences here have been rich and wonderful.

This Old House

It was impossible to resist the 1900 vintage edifice. One look at Atlin Lake from the ten-foot-high living room window and a glance at the tower soaring fifty feet over the street had us instant victims of its austere charm. So it was that one summer day nearly six years ago, we found ourselves the happy owners of this old house, Atlin's Old Government Building.

This old house stands fifty feet square and two stories high on Second Street where it was neatly rolled from its original place on the street behind some eighteen years ago. That is when the Provincial Government deemed it was too big and burdensome and ended its public life by abandoning it for a squat and unimposing pre-fab. It stood alone for twelve long years looking with the forlorn and vacant stare of all old buildings at the mountains and the passersby.

The Old Government Building has always commanded attention, and after we began repairs prior to moving in, we found tourists wandering in to ask what it was—an old school? —an old church? "They don't build 'em like this anymore," was one guy's comment as he pounded on the newel post. "Look, it's real wood." And many times, since that first summer, I have boosted complete strangers up through the trap door in my hall so they could take a picture from the tower window or just see what it's like up there. One night a handsome young constable from Teslin asked hopefully, "Is this where the dance is?"

Downstairs, the ceilings rise fourteen feet high. On the north side of the cavernous hallway is the courtroom. Here the judge's platform is framed in dark wood and His Worship looked down at those gathered in the somber gray room and made right the crimes of Atlin.

A small cubicle that served as the judge's chamber (or more often as cloakroom or library) has a faded and worn red carpet, a small offer of luxury to a traveling frontier judge.

In the Gold Commissioner's office, you think of the men who worked there. J.A. Frasier held that influential post from 1902 until 1922 when Atlin was a thriving gold mining town. In the mining recording office, there is a long and handsome wooden counter. Here, all government business was transacted, and over this counter poured documents for water rights, homesteads, timber leases, fur royalties, and the everlasting torrent of mining claims.

All summer I listen to visitors tell me how they envy me living in such a fascinating old place. I could tell them lots of things about living in an old building, but people steeped in romantic articles about preserving the past and saving historic sites and the current rage of resurrecting decaying barns and calling them home are not interested in the nitty gritty of living in an antique. They'd never believe it anyway.

Moving into this old house meant first repairing 52 broken windowpanes. That was nearly 300 pounds of glass. It also meant crawling on stomach and elbows the entire perimeter of the place just under the eaves and stuffing in insulation to ward off icy winds, which those same eaves trap so efficiently. It means to let a puppy out to piddle in the winter, you must first don parka, boots, and gloves, then sprint down twenty-five steps along an endless hallway to open the front door, praying all the way you won't get there too late.

We don't heat the downstairs except occasionally. With ceilings six feet higher than normal we would be heating about 15,000 cubic feet of space we couldn't even enjoy without a tall step ladder.

Years ago, a Gold Commissioner's wife became claustrophobic because there were only three windows in the entire upstairs. Soon four dormer windows were added. This improved the lighting, but the remodelers neglected the fact that they were altering the distribution of the roof load and in due time, the building developed some noticeable sags. Now, if you drop a marble on the floor, it can't decide which way to roll.

Under each of the four eaves is a huge L-shaped space. Three of these are closets, the fourth a pantry. The closets are the slanting ceiling, deep, mysterious kind that grandmother use to have that hint of rare and valuable treasures. The only thing worse than too little closet space is too much. These things become nightmarish catch-alls that are so darned handy they gobble up tons of miscellaneous items. Until they are someday cleaned out, I have learned to live without countless things that have become hopelessly lost within.

The bathroom facilities we found in this old building were quite unusual. In a very narrow room directly off the kitchen was a long, deep tub standing on four-clawed feet and a tiny oval washbasin. But where was the john? We discovered in a strange little room with a low doorway and ceiling that sloped from eight feet high on one side to two feet at the other. The whole room is suspended grandly over the landing of the stairway. To reach it you must walk through the entire pantry and if a tall man doesn't get brained on the door casing, he will surely thump his head on the slanting ceiling.

The bathroom, along with the dormers, electrical wiring, and for that matter, the kitchen were obviously afterthoughts. Originally the building had three staff rooms upstairs. It was probably the evolution of Atlin from mining camp to permanent town and a Gold Commissioner with a family that brought about the upstairs apartment and the "modern" innovations. One thing we never did find was the water system. Apparently, it was left behind on Third Street when the building was moved.

This old house will be seventy-three years old this year. It served Atlin during its youthful heyday, then watched sadly as the town declined. Now in a fresh coat of paint, it stands watching Atlin experience a reawakening and a quiet but steady boom quite different from its first gold rush excitement but probably one of longer duration. If this old house could tell its own life story, what an Atlin history we would have!

Many people here have flowers around their homes. We all love the splash of color after a long, white winter. As well as the weather being a constant nemesis, the horses and cows love flowers, too. This area of British Columbia is designated free-range, meaning livestock is free to roam anywhere it chooses. This is done to help augment the high cost of feed for the animals. It allows them to roam and feed themselves most of the year. The outfitters and ranchers have to feed them in the dead of winter but otherwise they fend for themselves much to the chagrin of many gardeners and flower growers. I do have to say, the tourists get a big kick seeing a herd of horses wandering down Main Street.

Porcupine Bites Dog

It is commonly known that dogs are quite prone to chasing and attacking porcupines, although it is a useless, prickly, and painful business. But this summer, so brazen have the porcupines become that they are now attacking the dogs.

Aishihik, a husky owned by Lance and Leah Fuller, can never tell what actually happened late one-night last week

17

at McKee Creek, but the facts are this. He was chained securely for the night at his doghouse. All was well. In the morning, Aishihik was still chained but he was sporting a full face of quills that was painful to look upon. The evidence is circumstantial; the deductions obvious. A porcupine discovered the captive dog and made the most of a good situation. Porky baited dog. Dog, of course, bit at the bait. That the bait was the porky himself was unfortunate for the dog. Sorry we can't report the culprit was apprehended and duly punished, but he made a clean get-a-way. No doubt he giggled all the way home at this slick turn of events.

Aishihik was dequilled the next morning. That brings to mind there is a present demand in Atlin for a good formula for removing quills from dogs when there is no veterinarian handy with a knock-out shot.

The stories revolving around quill-skewered dogs and the battles to dequill them are too many to count. The recipes for dequilling range from the ridiculous to the sublime—mostly ridiculous. I have asked my slobbering husky to hold his mouth open while I dab vinegar on quills impaling his tongue and jammed to the hilt between his teeth so they will soften up. I was fixed with such an evil-laden look, I withdrew directly and threw the swab away. "See, Rover, I threw it away."

I have tried, ever so gently, to clip the ends of the quills so they would deflate and be easier to pull. Deflate, my foot!

The first wave of the scissors turned my quill-filled husky into a canine Mr. Hyde who backed into a corner and snarled the blackest murder at me.

There have been tried tranquilizers that wouldn't tranquilize and sleeping pills didn't even make him yawn. And we have used elaborate and diabolical schemes of straight-jacketing to hold him immobile. But do you realize a medium-sized husky with a snoot full of quills can break shackles an enraged elephant couldn't budge?

There is a way, however, and the equipment needed is simple. Here it is.

Recipe for dequilling a husky:

One pair of pliers.

Four of Atlin's largest, strongest men.

Ear plugs are optional.

In the largest room in the house, move back all furniture and breakable items. Also remove rug. Lead dog to center of clearing. When he is off guard, flop him on his side on the floor. First strong man holds back legs. Second strong man holds front legs. Third strong man grabs dog by the throat and strangles him slightly. The fourth guy pulls the quills. When done on one side, flop flip over and do the other side. By then, dog is so exhausted he will open his mouth so you can pull the quills in there too.

When finished, the dog will sit up, scratch a little and walk casually outside. The men usually retreat to the bar.

Although this method of dequilling sounds brutal, it does work and the dogs actually don't mind much. In fact, I have heard of some dogs that will run right after another porcupine so that they can go through it all again. In the long run, the dogs usually hold up very well. Whether or not Atlin's largest, strongest men will, remains to be seen.

It's trapping season again, and a few early birds have sets out. We can't get to our line unless we get a boat until the lake freezes over. I'm hoping the cold air doesn't aggravate my bronchial asthma. I guess I can always bundle up and ride in the sled and leave the mushing to my husband. We'll have eight pulling dogs this winter so I won't feel like I'm imposing if I ride in the sled. It is annoying not being able to enjoy the out of doors like I used to. I never was much of a spectator, always wanted to be in on the action but can't complain much. At least I'm in the country I like, doing what I like, so that's half the battle.

The Trapper Always Gets Skinned

Trappers and gamblers suffer from the same enigma. Addicted to the game while cursing it, knowing the odds are stacked against them, still they go back for more hoping one day to come out the winner. The gambler pits his luck against the rolling dice or turn of a card but the trapper plays against more formidable odds that plague him from the time he first sets foot on the trapline in early winter until the fur checks come dribbling in during the waning days of spring.

How so? Isn't the life of the trapper independent, free, and virtually reeking of the romantic aura of the mountain men? Could be—but you can't buy traps and grub with intangibles though probably it is the love of independence and the outdoors that lures him back to his line again and again. Even so, years of low fur prices and tough competition from fur farms has thinned the ranks of the trappers leaving mostly those who would have no other kind of life.

This winter, fur prices soared higher than in two or three decades. The trapping season was longer and the rabbit cycle peeked during a relatively mild winter. There was a bumper crop of fox, lynx, and coyotes, and lots of wolves, if you could find them. Altogether it was a happy combination of circumstances the trappers haven't enjoyed for longer than memory.

The usual lot of trappers is quite different, however. His work is hard and there isn't much going for him anymore. He is a loner who spends weeks at a time out of touch with people. The chance he will wind up his trapping with enough cash to last him through the summer is slim. He plays against the odds and one of the worst is the weather. Weather can make or break his season. Seldom does the sun shine warmly upon the trapper, and if by chance it should, he can be sure to find all of his sets solidly frozen in the next time he checks his line. Extreme cold will keep him penned up in his cabin. Snow and wind obliterate his trails and cover his traps. Rain and sleet are worse. If he travels by snow machine, the cold will sabotage his engine. Sometimes the fickle thing will quit him entirely. Disgruntled is the trapper who has to trudge several chilly miles home leaving a sulking, sick machine beside the trail.

A dog team will seldom quit its trapper but dogs have other tricks just as aggravating. They love nothing better than a good brawl particularly when done up in several yards of dog harness. They also have a special penchant for sticking their feet into #4 traps and eating holes in unattended furs. Otherwise, they spend their spare time eating the trapper out of house and home.

The snowshoe trapper may have fewer transportation expenses but he will also be working a shorter trapline. His misery may run to blistered toes and mal de raquette, the shin shingles which can only be compared to square dancing with compound fractures in both legs.

A new affliction burdens the trapper and, if he be a sensitive soul, it may weigh on his mind a bit. In the eyes of the city conservationist, he has, of recent years, become a monster in the form of a Dracula who descends upon endangered species with diabolic, cunning intent on wiping them from the earth. Unknown, of course, to the armchair saviors of flora and fauna is that most trappers are practicing conservationists. They are quite familiar with the potential of their lines and are careful not to over trap. Doing so would effectively ruin an annual winter income. Working with the trapper also is the Game Department keeping tabs on fur yields and establishing controls when needed. Unknown also to those who would malign the trapper while eagerly buying and wearing his furs, is that the northern part of their country is a world apart. Life is different. Jobs are different. Trapping is still a business and part of the nation's economy. For many northerners, it is their only winter income.

So, unpopular with many because of the work he has chosen, the trapper nevertheless goes about his solitary business, gathering the furs needed to meet growing public demands.

Then, when the furs are stretched, turned, bundled, and labeled, he sends them off to the fur market. And here, at last, he faces the greatest odds of all. The promises made by the markets at the beginning of the season are suddenly bubbles bursting in the air. Number one demon of the market is undoubtedly the fur grader who must surely be instructed under threats of torturous death to never, never grade any fur Number One Prime . . . or for that matter, anything relatively close. The trapper wonders forlornly what mysterious things happen between the times his deeply pelted, extra-large furs are shopped and the grader gets hold of them. Somehow his furs must deteriorate and shrink at a rapid rate all the way to the market. And the long-awaited checks also shrink from what he imagined they would be when the season started and hopes were high.

Now the trapper goes off looking for a summer job. He needs to make ends meet and to accumulate a bit of a stake. He just can't wait to get back in the game again next winter.

She is a real outdoor gal. This winter, she and her older brother, Mike, are running a trapline just north of town. They have about five miles to go each way on their trapline now and will be adding more trail and traps right along. I gave her a puppy last winter, a half German Shepherd, half Siberian husky male. She taught the dog to pull and pack and this winter my husband rigged her small toboggan with handlebars so she could use the dog to pull her gear and sometimes herself around the trapline. It was obvious right away that she needed more dog power so I loaned her a Siberian of ours.

Lorrina: Trapper and Dog Musher

One cold day, a year ago, a slender, dark-haired girl and her younger brother were carefully making their way across a frozen lake two miles north of Atlin. Mike broke trail on snowshoes while close behind Lorrina walked in his tracks. At her heels followed two dogs, Timber and Cassiar, hauling a toboggan with a small cargo of trapping gear. It was twenty below.

Suddenly there was the sickening crack of shattering ice, and in that instant, Lorrina, dogs, and toboggan plunged through the deceptive overflow into a foot of frigid water. The terrified dogs, instinctively trying to protect their feet, pulled their paws up underneath themselves and lay flat and shaken on the fragile ice. Mike quickly tramped a trail to shore then walked cautiously back and threw the snowshoes to Lorrina. There was no other way for her to negotiate the thin ice during the nightmare job of getting dogs and toboggan off of the lake. But already the insidious water was seeping into Lorrina's mukluks.

Working against the inevitable danger of frozen feet and handicapped further because the frightened Cassiar refused to work, Lorrina pulled with Timber and slowly moved the toboggan, heavily encrusted with unyielding ice, to the beach where Mike already had a fire burning.

The dog's feet were dangerously iced but something told them to paw furiously in the dry pine needles under the trees and soon they freed themselves of the disabling ice.

Lorrina, using her axe, battered the ice from the toboggan's sliding surface. Then, not realizing her mukluks were thoroughly wet, she and Mike hitched up the dogs and headed swiftly back to Atlin.

What followed for Lorrina is the unfortunate tale of many a sourdough: the excruciating pain as her frozen feet thawed, the restless days limping tenderly around the house as the slow healing process took place, and worse, the gnawing thought of her trapline going unattended during the best part of the fur season.

Lorrina Price, at sixteen, is an accomplished trapper. She caught her first small fur bearer five years ago, and since that time, she has trapped each winter for the market. The furs she sells are well skinned and professionally stretched.

Last year, Lorrina, Mike, and another younger brother, Carl, worked the trapline north of town. Early in the season, Lorrina discovered that Timber, the only trained dog she had for pulling her toboggan, was not enough. Someone always had to walk, and checking the traps was a time-consuming business. Then someone loaned her a second dog, and with two dogs working, she could make the trip faster but was still under-powered. She borrowed another dog and then a couple more. Soon she was managing five or six rambunctious sled animals with reasonable skill. The work on the line had been cut in half, and the challenge of driving dogs had captured her. She decided that for her traveling by dog team was the only way to go.

Working during the summer with a training cart, Lorrina continued with Timber's lessons. Soon he was geeing and hawing, and generally working well ahead of the three other dogs she had acquired: Taku, a snowy Samoyed, Akala, a handsome, burly malamute, and speedy little Trapper, a fireball of mixed husky background.

Timber, she admits, is stubborn, but, by the same token, he is willing to bow to a superior force. He is half German shepherd and half Siberian husky. His German ancestry comes on strong in appearance and temperament, but his Russian half is all sled dog.

When there is pulling to be done, Timber is more than willing. He proved this fact quite effectively at an impromptu one-dog pull at the Atlin Fun Day last April. At Lorrina's command, he literally dug in and pulled a freight sled full of squirming kids from a dead stop over a course of sticky spring snow. This was an estimated 500 pounds—a surprising accomplishment for a dog just a year old. He had never been asked to do a job of this sort before.

Things are going smoothly on the trapline this winter. Lorrina's four dogs and two loaners, Kenai and Cassiar, are eager and well behaved, for the most part. She realized how much her team had improved when she hitched a new dog with them one day and discovered it was much like running with one flat tire.

For Lorrina, trapping is a business; the money made from her furs pays for her clothes and incidentals, food and rigging for the dogs, and of course, some must go back into traps. So, this winter when she found that an otter had blundered into one of her beaver sets, her mind automatically registered sixty dollars. The animal had to be clubbed and it kept disappearing beneath the creek ice. Each time it vanished she saw the hard-won sixty dollars slipping away. Since there was not enough snow on the trail for the team that day, she could also imagine an eight-mile hike for nothing. Happily, she got the otter and it counts among the numerous lynx and beaver and several mink and marten she has scored so far this season.

Although a competent trapper and woodsman, Lorrina, by law, is not old enough to carry a rifle with her on the trapline. This presents problems with which the other trappers of the area, all men, need not concern themselves. If an animal is found alive in a trap, she has to kill it. She must use a pole. "The longest pole I can find," she said. So far there have been no mishaps, but a potentially dangerous situation is always at hand. Someday she may find a live wolverine in a trap. Here would be a $100 fur wrapped around a notoriously vicious animal. The prospect of approaching this valuable but menacing creature armed only with a pole puts a burden on the young trapper the others need not consider. What would you do? Turn away from $100 or take your chance with a club?

The Number 4 trap is the largest and toughest of the commonly used flat traps. It is set for beaver, wolverine, and formerly it was used for wolves. Most men, but not all, can set a Number 4 by breaking it open over a knee. Lorrina sets hers this way. But it took a long time to learn this trick. She said, "It used to take three of us—one on each spring and one in the middle praying like mad no one else would let go!"

This winter, along with regular trips to the trapline, Lorrina is taking advantage of every free afternoon to work with her team. She has decided that her working dogs may very well double as racing dogs. On their days off, she runs them 12 or 14 miles against the clock, noting with great enthusiasm they are getting faster.

Lorrina carries a wicked looking, twelve-foot bullwhip on her sled. The dogs never feel its sting unless they fight. She uses it mainly to get their attention when they begin to doddle. When it whistles overhead and pops loudly nearby, the most delinquent dog quickly snaps to.

One day the whip got her into a ticklish situation. She had given it two mighty swings around her head to get the loitering dogs into action. But on the second circuit, the whip neatly picked the toque off her head and sent it flying into the air. It landed in the trail about twenty feet behind the sled, while up front, six highly-spooked dogs were raring to go. It wasn't easy convincing them they should "hold" while she gingerly walked back to retrieve her cap. It's always embarrassing for a musher to come home on foot.

Lorrina is going to try racing January 28 in Whitehorse when the Yukon Dog Mushers hold one of their scheduled races over a twelve-mile course. Then, at the end of February, the big one! The Sourdough Rendezvous in Whitehorse—three days of hard racing over a fifteen-mile course. Lorrina will be pitting her team and skill against other new mushers and veteran dog drivers, a big order for a sixteen-year-old girl, but one she will surely handle with a tough determination and casual good humor. Very important to this town is that this bright, fleet-footed girl and her dogs will be the first representatives that Atlin has ever had in the big Yukon race.

Now she is driving four dogs, and just a few minutes ago, she and Mike took off on their 10-mile jaunt. Kids are tough creatures but just the same, I gave them an extra parka and blanket and made sure they have plenty of matches along. I'll keep track of the time, and if they don't come back in the usual four or five hours, we'll send a snow machine out after them.

One Girl's Dog Sled Race

It was a cloudy, ten-below morning in Whitehorse. A sparse, shivering crowd lined the fences along the Yukon River. They stomped mukluks and waited while 19 dog teams assembled on the ice. It was the first day of the 1973 Yukon Championship Dog Sled Race.

Lorrina Price, Atlin's 16-year-old trapper, dog musher, and now race driver, waited, too. With just one 12-mile competition, her sole store of racing experience, she was about to match her six working dogs against a formidable field of seasoned teams and men mushers.

There was "Iron Man" Wilfred Charley of Carmacks, famed for his fumbling starts and flashy finishes. Wilfred had won the championship four times and was defending the title this year. Stephen Frost, dashing musher from Old Crow, has raced in every Rendezvous since 1962. He nabbed the title once and is consistently among the top five contenders.

Ed Bauman, cool, calm, and easy with his dogs, was a new face. He held an impressive string of wins during the pre-Rendezvous races. He was a new musher entering his first Championship Race. He proved his prowess as a musher by urging his huskies on to the coveted 1973 title. Unusual too, was the fact he finished first in each of the three-day heats and walked away with $800.00 for best aggregate time as well as the $450.00 day money.

Then there was "Loose Belt," Bob Erlam, publisher of the *Atlin News Miner* and the *Whitehorse Star*. Bob was the oldest musher in the race; Lorrina, the youngest, and between them, they waged a good-natured feud during the entire event. In the end, it cost Bob a big box of chocolates because Lorrina beat him in each of the three 15-mile races.

There were four tough contenders from Fort Nelson, British Columbia, and Nick Molofy was there with his team from Edmonton, Alberta. Molofy took the title to Alberta two different years and he still holds the track record of 55 minutes 51 seconds. One Bauman came close to breaking on the first day of the races.

Then Lorrina experienced the stomach-knotting tremors all racers encounter just before the "go" signal. She was in the starting shoot, sled tied to the snubbing post, her mother, Joan, acting as handler, held Trapper and Taku, the lead dogs. "15 seconds," the Starter yelled.

Trapper, who is usually screaming to be off, sat placidly surveying the spectators. Taku contemplated a spot on the snow. "10 seconds," came the ominous warning. Get up, Trapper. "9" The countdown started. "8-7-6..." Joan stepped away from the team. "5-4-3..." Akala looked vaguely interested but Cassiar and Kenia were yawning. Get up, Trapper! "2-1-mush." "Hike, Trapper, Hike."

He was up, they were all up and running, not full out but dead on the trail going the easy lope they use to cover the trapline. It was this steady lope and Lorrina's skill that brought her novice racers in with good respectable times in each of the three 15-mile heats: (1hr, 17min) (1:20:36), (1:20:49). Her consistent pace also won her $35.00 each day for finishing within 40 minutes of the winning team. She managed to cut this margin in half.

Lorrina's small team of work dogs range greatly in size and age. Taku, a registered Samoyed weighs 45 pounds—a good racing weight. Trapper, bright and fast, is a yearling. Usually, dogs aren't considered adult enough to race until they reach their second year. In wheel position is big Akala, a registered Malamute weighing 90 pounds. He works next to Kenai, a registered Siberian of the Seppala line who is over six years old. Another old-timer is Cassiar, a Malamute-Siberian and blind in one eye. He works point position with Timber, Lorrina's first sled dog, a Siberian-German Shepherd cross.

Lorrina's comments on the race shed light on some of the advantages and difficulties her "soup to nuts" team offered. She found the four-mile uphill stretch hard. Where the larger teams could take the grade at a lope with their drivers riding the runners, Lorrina did a lot of running to give the dogs a break. When she climbed aboard the team slowed, but big Akala kept things moving ahead anyway when he threw his weight into the harness.

Lorrina's dogs do a lot of traveling on Atlin Lake and are

familiar with ice. When she hit the river four-mile home stretch, she could keep her dogs at a fast run and gain valuable time. Other teams unused to the ice, spooked somewhat or missed the interest a trail offers and slowed to a trot.

Trapper picked his trail on a pre-run of the course and during the three heats, stuck stubbornly to avoid overflow and other distractions that caused trouble for some of the other drivers. The dogs passed other teams easily and went obediently around a pile up of teams near the starting line on the third day.

Lorrina plans to race again next year. She wants to try some of the other competitions around the north. She plans to run a larger team of better-matched and faster dogs. In the future, as the Yukon Championship Race just past, it is a good bet Lorrina will continue to capture the attention and admiration of those who see her. And win, lose, or draw, she will always be Atlin's Number-One Dog Musher.

Winters here are long and cold, but exciting and beautiful. We are surrounded by gorgeous scenery—towering mountains and the lake on which Atlin is situated is the largest in British Columbia. Today is one of those beautiful ones that make up for the shivery sixty-below zero we often have. Atlin Mountain, five miles across the lake, seems close enough to touch from my living room window. Tomorrow, we will be hitching up the dog team and going 12 miles down and across the lake to our trapline cabin to spend a week. For us, the trapping takes second place to the fun of getting out of town and enjoying the runs with the dogs along the shore.

The "Dry" Facts on Curling

The origin of curling is not known for sure. Some think the Flemings originated the game and in Teslin, they are positive this is true.

The Scots have been credited with sophisticating the game and with spreading its popularity to other countries. The Flemings are credited with spreading its popularity up and down the entire Alaska Highway.

It is known the Scots curled early in the 16th century. They called the stones "kuting stones" or "loofies." Nowadays, Atlin curlers have other names for the stones but they can't be printed in the *News Miner.*

A Scottish museum displays one stone which bears the date 1510. Atlin used to have an old stone that dated to the gold rush. It rested for years on the front porch of the Government Building. When the Atlin Curling Club held its first Gold Nugget Bonspiel in 1967, Tom Connolly was awarded this stone for some feat or other. No one told Tom it was all a big joke and he thought it would make a nice addition to his new fireplace. He cemented it securely and prominently into the fireplace facade. When he found he couldn't keep the stone, he had to chip the darned thing loose and it left an unsightly scar in his masonry. For some reason, that stone has never been seen again.

The very first curling stones were water-worn boulders with natural holes for thumb and fingers. Later on, handles were added, much to the delight of curlers who no longer had to wear steel-toed shoes.

Some of the early stones weighed over a hundred pounds. They were in use before the advent of the Bonspiel. As its popularity grew, the heavy stones were abandoned in favor of stones weighing about 40 pounds. This prevented curlers from becoming exhausted with playing the game and left them more energy for Bonspieling.

The first curling games were played on natural ice on ponds or lakes. However, cold weather and the need to play during the daytime time soon led to the building of covered rinks. The First Gold Nugget Bonspiel was played on the slough near the Atlin Street Bridge. At this outdoor event, coldness and lack of light were remedied with Moosemilk and artificial lighting. Although this worked very effectively, the Atlin Curling Club built a covered rink anyway in which artificial lighting was installed. The problems of cold and light were solved but the popularity of Moosemilk and similar things like, Sluice Spiel Spunch prevailed when it was found they were great for dispelling the gloom of losing or to celebrate a hard-fought victory.

Canada was one of the early followers of curling, and in 1852, the first Canadian branch of the Royal Caledonian Curling Club was established. The present Atlin Curling Club was established in 1967 and since has grown in membership and flourished as one of Atlin's most active organizations. It is probably safe to predict that this club will continue hale and hardy as long as curling and Moosemilk exist.

Right now we have lots of snow, beautiful crystal-clear days, and nippy ten-below nights. It is so pretty here. I appreciate our little spot in the woods even more after seeing once again the smog and heaving humanity in southern California and points south. Sometimes we get the feeling the world has passed us by, left us without the nice things like running water and flush toilets, etc. But I'll trot off happily to my little gray outhouse forever as long as we don't get overrun by freeways, concrete sidewalks, and the mash of people that go with it all.

A Mystery of Merit

It was a moonless night in early October when Ben Able turned down the Atlin Road from the Alaska Highway. His 1959 4x4 pickup truck bumped along the gravel and Ben had only 60 more miles to Atlin and home. Suddenly his mind came alert. Someone was standing in the fireweed stubble just off the right-hand side of the road. The pickup passed and Ben looked through the side window directly at a slim figure not more than 10 feet away. Strangely its head did not turn to follow the passing pickup but instead faced straight toward the road.

Thinking someone wanted a ride or needed help, Ben stopped and backed up a little past where the figure had first stood. By now it had moved away and was about 20 to 25 feet off the road in the dim side light cast off by the head lamps. Its head was turned in profile. Ben turned off his truck engine and got out to stand in the door well. He spoke across the top of the cab. "Are you in trouble? Do you need a lift?" There was no answer and no movement. For a full 5 minutes, Ben watched the quiet figure then he saw it move away past a small jack pine tree and out of site into the bush. There was no sound.

Ben got back in his truck and continued on the road to Atlin. It was then that the full impact of what he had just seen struck him. His mind reviewed the scene. The headlights had been full on the figure when he first passed it. The color he remembers seeing was a bluish hue. "Like a Russian Blue cat." It seemed small—perhaps the size of a boy about 5½ feet tall. The face was gray. Features were vague. Only gray fingers of the hands were exposed. The arms seemed very long. Hair swept back and up from the forehead but there was fur close under the chin and all down the body. When the creature was farther away, after Ben backed up to offer help, its color seemed to blend into the dimly lit night. In profile, the back of the head had a definite forward slope. When it went away into the woods, its motion was smooth. There was no bobbing movement at all.

There are a few Indian and white people living in the immediate area and often there are hitchhikers on the Atlin Road, though seldom at 10:30 at night. Nevertheless, someone could have been out after dark. But almost any human will answer a direct question. Seldom does a human view a passing object without turning its head to follow the movement. And it is unlikely a person would walk off into the bush at night where there is no house or other logical place to go. Also, humans have a certain bouncy gate. They do not glide smoothly along.

Considering things real and unreal, there seemed only one word to explain what Ben had seen and the word, Sasquatch, hit his mind like a small anticlimactic bomb. Ben was immediately irritated almost angry with himself. He had both a spotlight and a camera among his effects in the pickup. Perhaps a great mystery might have been solved that night. But then few rational men ever, expect to encounter a Sasquatch nor would they be prepared if they did.

Since October 4, Ben Able has answered a lot of questions about what he saw on the Atlin Road. Did it have the strong objectionable odor said to accompany some Sasquatch? No. Did he ever go back and look for prints? Yes. He was at the site several days later. Freezing weather and hard gravel made the rights of way bordering the road impervious to prints. Was there any sound from the creature? None at all. Could it have been a bear? No. Ben was born in Dawson Creek. He is a heavy equipment operator and a miner who has spent a great part of his life in the bush in close company with bears. He'd know one if he saw it. Was he afraid? No. Ben wasn't afraid but he was entirely amazed at what he'd seen. He was so astounded, in fact, he was prompted to formally relate his story the next day to Corporal Mike Morhun of the Atlin RCMP detachment.

At first Ben was hesitant about having his experience written, but later related it to this reporter advising that it be written factually. As usual, when accounts deal with age-old mysteries, the reader reaches the last lines and finds himself waiting for the second boot to hit the floor. There is nothing more to add to Ben's episode. There are no conclusions to be drawn that will reveal the Sasquatch mystery. Only theories and suppositions may be made.

If you feel frustrated, you are in league with hundreds. Some men have spent endless hours and great amounts of money trying to crack the Sasquatch case. Sightings of Sasquatch or Sasquatch-like creatures have been recorded since the early half of the 1800s and come from all corners of the world. One author compiled impressive records of sightings and foot prints, but he told of only two Yukon sightings. British Columbia, Washington, Oregon, and California lead the field, and the density of sightings corresponds conspicuously with the density of human population.

Men of reliable scientific backgrounds have dipped into the realm of the Sasquatch. Government money backed one American researcher. Volumes of data have been compiled but no one researcher, hunter, or sighter has produced completely credible proof for or against the Sasquatch.

Perhaps many who have given more than casual thought to the question of Sasquatch feel the same as Dr Maynard Miller, noted glaciologist and geologist. He once told me that he hoped there really were Sasquatch and that no one ever caught one.

This is a very busy weekend—Victoria Day—three days of fun and sun for all but us working stiffs. Atlin is chucked full of people. Most of them down from Whitehorse—lots of youngsters came down for a dance held last night. It is sort of country western-ish usually but we get some exceptionally good musicians who come here to play for nothing just because they like our little town. We had the British Columbia and Yukon fiddle playing champions. They are a real draw.

The Way It Used to Be

Dog sled racing is a tough sport today. Interest has increased tremendously over the last few years, and as more people move into the racing circle, the tracks become longer and harder, but, by the same token, the winners' purses become fatter.

The Yukon Championship Race in Whitehorse is a 45-miler with 15-mile heats over three days. It draws 20 teams now as compared with six when it was first held ten years ago.

The World Championship Race held in Anchorage, Alaska, draws the crack teams from the lower forty-eight, Canada, Europe, and Alaska. To win this race, as George Attla, an Athabascan Indian from Husila, Alaska, has done several times, you drive a team of 16 dogs that cruise at 15 miles an hour. This speed wins the Yukon race. Then you urge these dogs to hit speeds of 20 miles per hour in the final grueling home stretch.

Most of this race track is within the city limits of Anchorage, through streets lined with cars and surging with spectators—bad enough for dogs from the bush, but worse yet, they must run on concrete covered with a hauled-in blanket of snow. This is a race to tax the physical and mental limits of both team and driver—a test of endurance and skill.

But I wonder what the mushers of yesteryear would think of our races today. How about men like Leonard Seppala, the diminutive Norwegian who ran the socks off every team in Alaska, and in doing so, made the Siberian husky famous? Seppala won his first racing notoriety by winning the All Alaska Sweepstakes in 1915 at Nome. This race was a 408-mile round trip between Nome on the Bering Sea and Candle, Alaska, on the Arctic Ocean. His time in that classic event was 81 hours, 3 minutes and 45 seconds—less than four days.

The course lay along the telephone line so messages raced back and forth and bulletins were posted in Nome so boosters could keep track of their favorite mushers. In a history of the races, Esther Birdsall Darling wrote, ". . . the town waits day and night for reports on the whereabouts and welfare of the racers." Strange spectator sport as compared with today's races where there is scarcely enough time to get a cup of coffee between take-off time and when the first team is sighted heading for the finish line.

The 408-mile race was sponsored by the Nome Kennel

Club and their members-maintained relay stations along the route where drivers and teams could get food and rest. The trick was to know how long you could stop without losing too much time. The only required stop was at Candle, where judges inspected the teams before they headed home on the second leg of the race.

The equipment the drivers carried on their sleds was furs and rubber boots for themselves and moccasins for the dogs. They also took dark veils for the dogs to prevent snow blindness. The drivers rarely rode in the sleds. The stood on the runners and pumped or ran behind pushing to help the dogs.

After Seppala won the 1915 All American, the townsfolk of Nome were proud when he received an invitation to compete in the Ruby Derby of 1916. The Ruby Race was considered one of the short ones, a marathon run over a 58-mile course. Seppala entered and won easily, but to do so he had to mush his team 450 miles over mountain passes along the frozen Yukon River and through sub-arctic forests to reach the town of Ruby.

Leonhard Seppala lived to be 89 years old and raced until nearly 60. He saw the modern-day mushers dashing off to races with their dogs loaded in neat camper kennels aboard comfortable pickup trucks or packed aboard swift airplanes. These sights must have brought vivid pictures of his own early racing days and his 450-mile trip by dog team just to reach the race course.

Probably there were times when Leonhard Seppala felt the same way Norman Fisher felt the other night. Norman, who is 89, put in hundreds of miles mushing the mail team from Carcross to Atlin and on to Telegraph Creek years ago. But after listening to an hour of high-powered dog talk at a table of mushers down at the Curling Club Lounge, he said quietly and with a twinkle, "You know, I decided I don't know anything about dogs."

The ice on the lake is full of open leads and looks quite black and uninviting. It should break up and disappear soon. The grass is turning green and leaves are just about to pop open on the bushes and trees. We had a town clean up last weekend. The whole town pitches in and helps clean up and prepare for summer. Afterwards, we have hot dogs and pop for the kids. All Altinites volunteer and it's quite an event, everyone participates. So when the ice goes out and summer officially begins, we are ready for visitors from near and far.

Something about a Dog

It would be easy to write a large volume about dogs. In fact, if I devoted just one chapter to each of the many dogs we have owned over the last fourteen years, my manuscript would equal *War and Peace* and *Gone with the Wind*. Thinking it over, either of those titles would be suitable for my dog book too.

For now, though, I'll just tell you something about one dog named Chilkoot. He is a sled dog whose interests vary greatly from those of his peers. I think it all started when Chilkoot was still a pup and received a cruel injury that undoubtedly influenced most of his future life.

One day, he tagged after an older dog who was out chasing women. He returned sometime later, head down and hurt badly. We determined he had been hit across the nose with what must have been a heavy club or board. Bones were broken, nasal passages crushed, and teeth broken. Probably some owner of a female dog was unhappy with the attentions of our malamutes.

After Dr. Cliff Loubough had carefully patched and wired him together, the only noticeable indication of the encounter was that Chilkoot turned his head aside if anyone reached to touch his face. Outwardly, he was intact but I always suspected his nose didn't work quite right again. For instance, he wasn't particularly interested in the springtime romancing most male dogs pursue with great enthusiasm. He was happy to putter around the house and yard instead, and eventually he developed a leaning toward things of a mechanical nature as a substitute for love in the spring.

Along regular lines were his lively interests in pickups and cars, mainly the tires. Once he got loose in a large parking lot, a place he rarely was able to visit, he squirted thirty-six tires before we chased him, hopping three-legged out of the place.

Chilkoot is a detached sort of animal, and his absent-mindedness, along with his unusual penchant for mechanical items, led into two collisions with pickup trucks. In fact, he ran into the trucks rather than the other way around. The first crash resulted in a hip injury that plagues him now in his golden years and shortened his career as a wheel dog on the team. The next time, he stuck his foot under a speeding pickup and had a fat and painful paw for several weeks.

Later on, it occurred to me he was probably trying to

squirt the tires of the moving vehicles to set some new record. He didn't try again, and, as far as I know, it has never been accomplished with any success.

Chilkoot liked handles, latches, and locks and has become expert at opening doors. He mastered most of the house doors wherever we lived and then learned to open the door of my car. The first time he let himself into my car I was keeping a female husky in it part of the time since it was spring and the male dogs were chasing women as usual. Young son was loudly blamed for carelessly leaving the door open, an accusation he strongly denied while no doubt wondering what the car door could possibly have to do with the black threat of unwanted puppies.

Chilkoot's motivations were not of a romantic nature, however. He just enjoyed pretty Kluane's company in any season and got in the car to pass a sunny afternoon. I am sure his lack of nose power had squelched his normal canine urge to blanket the world with pups.

Finally, we saw him open the door by hooking one broken fang under the latch to release it. The problem was he often invited his muddy cronies to join him and the mess they made in the car was complete. So, to foil his trick, I parked the car on a slant and locked the lower door. Minutes later, Chilkoot was sitting happily behind the wheel. He had unlatched the high side door then pulled it back enough to wiggle inside. His entrance was great, but exit he could not. When it was time to get out and check the tires, he had to bark for help.

After Chilkoot began spending a lot of time sitting in my car, it naturally followed that he should try to drive. The dashboard full of gadgets must have intrigued his technical brain and the idea of driving the car may have been one of the reasons he wanted in in the first place.

Anyway, one day he decided to drive down Discovery Street. First bumping it out of gear, he eased the car away from in front of the house and headed down the three-block-long hill leading to the lake. I think he would have made it all the way to the water if it had not been for Ron Bowden over at the garage, who saw what he was up to and didn't think he should be driving yet. He dashed across the street and jerked the door open so he could take the wheel. This really made Chilkoot cranky and he told Ron to bugger off ... wouldn't even let him ride along.

Ron figured it was best not to argue, even though Chilkoot didn't have many teeth left, so instead he came to tell me my dog was driving my car. In the meantime, the interruption had flustered Chilkoot and he veered across the road and into the corner of Rudy's property.

I was relieved my car hadn't ended up in the lake, but felt that Chilkoot should have been more apologetic about taking the car without asking. Instead, he just sat there scowling and muttering about Ron butting in.

Chilkoot is past ten years old now and he doesn't drive anymore. As a matter of fact, he never did get his driver's license. He did okay on the written exam but couldn't pass the driving test because he saw Ron on the road and got mad all over again.

Mostly Chilkoot sits in the car and waits for summer tourists who like to take pictures of him. But I've noticed something of late. Whenever a plane flies over, he leans out the window and watches it until it disappears from sight. And one day at the air strip, he hung around the parked planes instead of chasing squirrels like he usually does. Now, you don't suppose that silly old codger is going to try to . . .

We had a lot of fun here over the Dominion Day holiday. It is the first of July and our little town puts on a big do. We had a parade—not half bad for a bunch of amateurs—and a big dance and horse races, etc. And concession booths with carnival-type games for the kids at the campground, a large unimproved field at the end of town. The local children really enjoy all of this. Since they are not television kids, they look forward to each event with great anticipation. As usual, everything is done by volunteers.

The Tradition of the Latchstring

When the latchstring is out on the cabin door it means, "Welcome, stranger, be my guest. Use my cabin and help yourself to my supplies. I may have to call at your cabin sometime when you are away, and I will expect the same hospitality." But the symbolic unlocked cabin door has a deeper meaning. It signifies a faith in fellow northerners and cheechakos (newcomers to the north) as well and an interest in their well-being. It is a pledge that personal property be respected and that generosity is reciprocal. It is a northern tradition that in recent years has often been badly abused.

One winter night when the mercury lurked at minus fifty, a young man was driving the Atlin Road. He had arrived in Whitehorse that day by plane from Vancouver and had neglected to change to appropriate warm clothing before starting for Atlin. About sixteen miles from his destination, he succumbed to drowsiness and road hypnosis and his vehicle plunged into the deep snow at the side of the road. The billowing cascade filled his engine compartment and smothered the engine and it wouldn't start, so he could not use the heater. Two miles farther on was an emergency shelter, his only hope, and he made a desperate dash for it. Soon in its black interior, he fumbled with matches and wood and managed to start a lifesaving fire.

These shelters with their latchstrings always out were built and maintained by the Atlin highway crew. Their vital importance is recognized be Atlinites who travel the sixty-mile deserted Atlin Road in winter. Others are not so concerned and the next summer, windows and the stove were destroyed in one of the shelters. Why? Winnie Atcheson, Atlin correspondent for the Whitehorse Star, made a plea in her column that these buildings be respected and so they are by most. But her words fell on deaf ears of the pranksters, the weirdos, the sickies that find their way into the north.

One summer a man who was establishing a wilderness home for his family at the end of Atlin Lake cached food supplies at a friend's trapline cabin on the lake shore. Returning later to retrieve his goods, he discovered they had been stolen. Gone also were the cabin owner's lanterns and gas supply. None of these things were ever replaced. Why?

On the other hand, some Atlinites used this same cabin for a summer holiday. When they left, the cabin and grounds were clean and orderly, wood was stacked near the stove and food was ready for the next visitor. They understood the tradition of the latchstring.

As Atlin grows steadily in population, more residents are going off the beaten trails into the wild for various reasons. Some are trapping, others mining or prospecting. Still others are just looking for spots away from it all. Many have repaired abandoned cabins and registered them for taxes. Some have built new cabins. Each of these places is important to the owner. Each cabin is also important as an emergency shelter. Even a cabin suffering from disrepair could save the life of a lost or stranded man. Once, a man could leave his cabin vacant and unlocked for long periods secure in the knowledge it might be used but never abused.

Now a man leaves his place with certain misgivings. The latchstring is out, but he wonders how things will be when he returns. Often his fears are realized and he returns to a damaged cabin and pilfered belongings. Why? Certainly, the percentage of destruction-bent individuals is no greater than years ago. Maybe we are to blame because we have let the tradition of the latchstring drift into the dusty past when it should always be a part of the present. Maybe we should dig it out, dust it off, and put it back into use again. It is, after all, one of the best of the old northern traditions.

Last fall, my husband went to work in the northern Yukon on the Dempster Highway job. This is the road that will in due time loop from Whitehorse, Yukon to near Dawson City, then to Inuvik, Northwest Territories. From there, it will lead back to Edmonton, Alberta, making a long loop into the Arctic where we haven't been able to get to easily before. I'm planning a trip at the first possible moment. I'm really interested in seeing the tundra country.

Average Woman Atlin Variety

From the kitchen of a snug log house comes a loud thud and a smack. A quick look reveals a young woman with a smudge of flour on her cheek, dressed in jeans, and a blouse tails hanging out. She is expertly beating gobs of elastic brown dough into oblong shapes and popping them into pans. Soon they will emerge from her oven— beautiful, rich loaves of bread. A tendril of hair trails in one eye as the young woman turns to other chores. She slips outside to hang a large sign near her front door. It

51

says simply "Water." Then she sits down to agonize over a large stack of catalogs, making out orders for things she hopes will be sent quickly and correctly. Since she does about a fourth of her shopping by mail order, she knows well the black labyrinth of paperwork encountered if she has to return, reorder, or track down a missing item.

The flour-dusted face seen on this particular weekday morning is only one of many faces of the Average Woman, Atlin Variety. This young woman leads a life different than that of a stereotypical housewife and she often faces situations unknown in the predictable lives of her sister-city dwellers.

If she smokes, she probably rolls her own, but this act, usually associated with range-riding cowboys, loses all essence of masculinity in her hands. It is an economic measure.

To come here, she and her husband gave up jobs which provided a comfortable joint income. Now small savings make a sporadic income stretch farther.

Her closet is a variable paradox. A quick inventory would baffle her city sister. It might read something like this: One pair of muddy leather shoe packs, a beautiful mini-length dress, two or three pair of faded blue jeans, a stunning velveteen parka trimmed with wolf that she made herself, a pair of over-the-knee street boots and a pair of beaded mukluks. Her lingerie may be one-half frilly bikinis, one- half long johns. She wears sexy black pantyhose or gray wool socks with equal aplomb.

The Average Atlin Gal is an outdoor woman. She likes a riotous snowmobile ride over a moonlit lake. She may be learning the graceful swinging glide of cross-country skiing under the expert guidance of Francoise and Stephen Shearer, Atlin instructors and advocates of ski touring. She can hurl a forty-pound curling rock with fair accuracy and ease.

Although at this moment, she doesn't present a picture of glamour, if the occasion demands, the Average Atlin Woman can transform herself into a dazzling creature that could easily hold her own at any social function.

The Average Atlin Woman is somewhere under thirty and has two small children. One child may be a baby of less than a year since Atlin, which has long been omitted from the stork's itinerary, has suddenly become one of his prime targets.

The Average Atlin Woman is not Atlin born. She has been here less than five years and came originally from a heavily populated area. She and her husband abandoned their former home for a smaller town and larger wilderness. Atlin seemed a better environment for a growing family.

Atlin's Average Woman doesn't enjoy all the conveniences she took for granted in her city life. No tiled bathroom for her now. More than likely a small traditional building in the backyard has replaced the usual bathroom fixtures. The sign she hung out this morning is her assurance of a continuing water supply. It signals Ron Bowden, the water man, to fill her storage barrels. Running water and sewer systems are things of the past.

Our gal has acquired new skills since moving here. She drives a pickup truck with the same finesse she used to wheel her sedan through the five o'clock traffic. She is handy with an axe since her kitchen range is a wood burner. Although not a dead-eye shot yet, she sometimes bags a moose or caribou for the family freezer and she enjoys a lone horseback ride through the pines.

There are frustrations in her life. Fifty pounds of spuds freeze then thaw and run a black mess all over the pantry floor. Mud tracks in by the ton during the spring thaw. There are times of quiet apprehension. Her oldest kid goes out to play at twenty below. A lost mitten could mean a frozen hand. A tiny knot forms in her stomach when someone close is late coming home from Whitehorse on a minus-forty-degree night. The fire siren sounds and her blood runs cold. Vivid memories of Atlin fires crowd her brain. And when winter stretches long, the four walls may close in and cabin fever is near.

These times occupy a small part of her life and mostly she is too busy to be worried long. A glance at Atlin Mountain wreathed in morning mist can dispel cabin fever and a boisterous curling bout will make the time whiz by until the late arrival gets home.

It is evening now. The kids are ready for bed and a babysitter is settled in with her homework. There is a dance at the new Recreation Center tonight and it's almost time to go. Average Atlin Gal suddenly steps from the bedroom. Wow! Our floury mouth has become a glittering butterfly! Her new hairdo sparkles with gold dust. A stylish mini dress barely peeks below the velveteen parka. She wears mukluks and carries a pair of platform sandals. Her husband gives an appraising look at legs that are usually encased in jeans. Then she takes his arm and disappears into the crisp, white Atlin night.

Probably you know we are in the clutches of a nationwide postal strike here in Canada—going on four weeks now. It is a great inconvenience for us in faraway locations because we depend on the mail service for much of our existence. However, I really enjoy not having to pound out letters by the dozens each week or skittering off to the post office at the zero hour each mail day (three times weekly).

Evalyn's Boofus

"Have you visited The Boofus Shop?" "The what?" the tourist asked with a slight giggle and a fishy look at me. The Boofus, THE BOOFUS!" I repeated beginning to feel like I was doing a solo on a tuba. "What is it?" "Well, you'd better go and see for yourself," I said giving directions. Away went the tourist with an incredulous look on his face.

A snug little log cabin nestles under spreading cottonwoods on the corner of Third and Sinclair Streets in Atlin. A slab fence encircles it and two knobby burl logs hold up the porch roof. Over the door a rustic sign proclaims that this is indeed The Boofus Shop. Here is an unusual collection of gifts and souvenirs, most of them created by Evalyn Colwell who is the owner and operator of the little log shop with the funny name.

Evalyn's craft work covers a wide scope but her most popular items must certainly be her skillfully carved leather purses and wallets. She fills a continuous stream of orders for these and other leather things ranging from guitar straps to rifle scabbards to horse bell straps.

Evalyn began doing leather work several years ago to help pass the time while living in a strange town. Now it is hard finding time enough for her hobbies which have become a growing business.

She has worked away from most standard leather tooling patterns into designs of her own that reflect scenes peculiar only to Atlin, local game animals, and local sports. Happy is the curler who carries his mad money in a special The Boofus Shop wallet won as a prize at the Atlin Gold Nugget Bonspiel. Her carved animals are sharp and realistic probably because, as an ardent outdoorsman, Evalyn's has made close observation of all of them.

Evalyn and Harold Colwell first came to Atlin in 1959 not long after they were married. They were flown to the shore of Gladys Lake some miles out in the bush east of town. There they were dumped with gear and a canoe and for two and a half months, they prospected the Gladys Lake region on a government grubstake. The summer was cool, wet, and windy and the mosquitoes hungry, Evalyn recalls. They didn't find a mine but they saw endless beautiful country deserted for the most part since the passing of the early gold miners.

It was ten years later that the Colwell family, now including five children, left their home in Squamish, BC and headed north again to Atlin "because we'd always thought we would like to come back."

Three summers ago, Evalyn opened The Boofus Shop. Harold built the little cabin and Evalyn filled it with craft work. Evalyn views things through a craftsman's eyes. A strange little burl on a tree may become a unique toothpick or match holder. A larger burl makes the base for a rustic lamp. A bit of left-over leather becomes a sturdy case for camera gadgets.

Evalyn has been a rock hound for years. She has the special knowledge needed to separate the good rocks from the clunkers and she can proceed with cutting, shaping, and polishing to make a finished piece of jewelry, a pen stand, or some other unusual item from her active imagination.

The theme throughout is plainly evident. At The Boofus Shop you'll find northern gifts and souvenirs made nowhere else but in the north.

As for that name—Boofus—it's taken from Boofus Mountain which stands near the north shore of Gladys Lake. Maybe it was a lingering memory of Boofus Mountain blending with the striking Gladys Lake back country that brought the Colwells back to Atlin and eventually resulted in the founding of The Boofus Shop— the little log shop with the funny name.

The Boofus Shop

Gifts - Souvenirs
Atlin, B.C.

Atlin was and is a mining town. It had a rush for gold in 1898. Because this was during the Klondike gold rush which was so much bigger, Atlin's interesting golden history is almost unknown except to the few of us who found this lovely little nitch in the north. Sometimes I think most of us Atlinites are secretly glad we are in this little-known spot and hope it will stay small in population and free of the troubles big cities have.

We Love 'Em

Tourists come, in all sizes. Some are shapely and some are shapeless. They come from places like Kanazawa, Japan and Osoyoos, British Columbia. They come in long, low cars, muddy pickups, campers, and sometimes by boot or sneaker with pack sacks on their backs. Tourists come to Atlin in ever increasing numbers each summer and of the thousands of them plying the northern highways, we think the ones who find their way to Atlin are A-1.

People willing to drive sixty extra miles of gravel road to a very small town in a very large wilderness are going through a natural screening process. Only those really interested in what's at road's end will make the trip. Most of these travelers will reach us with a pretty good idea of what Atlin is all about. They have found bits of information in travel folders or current periodicals and want to fill in missing details. Some tourists are here today, then gone forever. Others return year after year. Some opt to stay and add their numbers to Atlin's growing population.

Some of our tourists, the young pack toters, have traveled the Alaska Highway using a thumb for main propulsion. They are searching for the back trails and places away from the mainstream of travel. They find Atlin large enough to furnish supplies but remote enough to have romantic intrigue.

Many of our tourists are sportsmen in search of big lake trout or tasty Arctic grayling. Others are guests of the four outfitters who hunt out of Atlin. Their quest is for big game and the hunting areas here annually produce outstanding trophies to satisfy the more selective hunter.

Often our tourists are retired and enjoying for the first-time, holidays within limits. Sometimes they stay here for weeks and become Atlinite's for a while before moving on.

Canadians account for two thirds of the travelers who reach Atlin. A lot of these should be listed as neighbors just dropping in to call because Whitehorse people are constant visitors and constitute a large segment of our summer trade. Americans, who begin to arrive in noticeable numbers in mid-June, are mainly from the coastal states but there is a good representation from northern and eastern states too. A small number of visitors hale from overseas. England, Wales, Japan, Norway, Denmark, Scotland, and Africa have all been represented this summer. Most of these folks were visiting relatives or friends in Whitehorse and were brought to Atlin for a scenic side trip.

Tourists have dozens of questions to ask. How cold are the winters? What do we do for a living? Are there many wolves? Do most of us live here all year round? Another question is frequently and plaintively asked. Do you think Atlin will change? Atlin is growing and our tourists worry that we might lose our heads in the quest for a better economy. They fear we may grow to quickly and loose the things they find appealing—the rugged frontier look of the town, our low-rise skyline that interferes not at all with the bold background scenery, the slow-going northern pace. Though not all visitors would care to experience the extreme cold winters or put up with the bother of having no water and sewer system, many think we live in a particular kind of Eden. They are glad they found this spot and we are happy to have shared it with them if only for a day.

**EVALYN COLWELL
CRAFTS FROM WOOD**

Well, it's time to scrub my young son. He is soaking in a galvanized tub in front of the oil heater. Since he is a big school boy now, we have to keep the dust and dirt washed off.

The Question and Answer Game

Although the tourists are a little scarce this summer, there are still enough of them here for me to indulge in one of my favorite summer pastimes: the Question and Answer Game.

After several years' practice, I should be showing some signs of expertise at the game, but each year someone throws me a curve and I lose points toward my amateur rating.

Most tourists who make it to Atlin already have a good idea of what the town is all about. At least they know Atlin is here because gold was discovered in Pine Creek back in 1898. But they are sometimes surprised to find some 400 hardy souls hacking out an existence in the British Columbia bush. Many expected to find a couple of crotchety old miners and a trapper or two.

Usually, travelers have heard of the marvelous scenery, but words can't justly describe it, so at first, they may be somewhat speechless and wide-eyed. This soon passes, however, and healthy curiosity takes over. This is the beginning of the Q/A Game.

Since I am mostly in my gift shop on summer days, I am one of the Atlinites who is a handy target for questions. These questions seem to fall into categories. There are the academic ones about Atlin history, flora and fauna, the town's economics or lack of it, and meteorology. I can usually bungle through history and I know who can fill them in on the plants and animals, but then comes the question that falls under economics. It is a stumper and it sounds like this: "Aaaa say, just what the hell do people do here to make a living?" The guys who ask this really want an answer, and do you know I haven't the foggiest idea what to tell them. I can't tell them this, of course, since it is apparent some 400 Atlin residents are getting along rather well with no visible means of support. . . . So I mutter a bit about mining and trapping and government jobs and hope this will be satisfactory. If they dig farther, I pretend to have a coughing fit and leave the shop. . . . Actually though, for ten solid years I have been looking for the answer to this question and haven't yet cracked it.

COME SHOP

• UNUSUAL GIFTS
• HANDMADE LEATHERWEAR
• ATLIN PLACER GOLD
• UNIQUE ATLIN CRAFTS
• JADE JEWELRY
• PRIME FURS

The DISCOVERY SHOP

P.O. BOX 96

There has to be something going on here that even I don't know about.

Another touchy area is the one listed directly under psychology, and it has to do with the dread affliction called cabin fever. The question comes in hushed tones . . . "Do people really get cabin fever?" They make it sound like a contagious, unmentionable disease. It is popular presently to call cabin fever the Arctic Madness and truthfully, I can't say whether we have it or not, all things being relative. . . . However, I suspect that most outsiders would agree it is running rampant even in the summertime.

Under weather is the inevitable . . . "How cold does it get here in the winter?" I don't really remember when it was last 60 below (Fahrenheit) or even 50 below, but to make the traveler happy I say casually that it drops to around 60 in the winter and sort of kick the floor nonchalantly as though I was stuffed with genuine eiderdown.

The fascination for gold never tarnishes, and I explain to people that we use real Atlin gold nuggets on the jewelry in my shop. But one time a guy came in and after several minutes of careful browsing he sidled up and whispered confidently, "What do you use for gold?" I never did convince him it was the real McCoy.

Another interesting question is one always accompanied by a leer . . . "What do you do during the long, dark winter nights?" That one is easy. I just leer back sweetly and say, "It's none of your darned business."

The question that requires an immediate, detailed answer always comes from a harassed woman from whose hand dangles a desperate child with crossed legs and eyes afloat. "Where is your bathroom?" she hisses.

"Lady, I haven't had a bathroom since I left civilization ten years ago. In fact, I don't even have a room where I could put a bath if I ever acquired one." Well, I don't really tell her this.

Instead, I direct her to the outhouse. "Outhouse?" Do you realize that at least 78 percent of the world's population does not know what an outhouse is? So, you can imagine the shock as the woman rounds the woodpile, threads her way through four or five husky dogs and finds—the place which I have had to translate into "bathroom" so she could understand me.

Well, after the initial surprises, I have noticed that almost all of our tourists manage our rustic conveniences with no major setbacks. In fact, they seem to get a kick out of roughing it with us for a while. And the fact that so many come back makes me think they have discovered something about Atlin while poking around and playing the Q/A Game. Maybe they find out that they possess a bit of the pioneer spirit required to exist in an out-of-the-way little town. Something must have made them drive the rather bumpy road to Atlin, and in the end, they fit in nicely with the scheme of things here.

This is the high part of the rabbit cycle and with lots of fox, coyote, lynx and the controversial wolf. The wolf is an interesting animal. They make good pets if tamed when pups; crossed with dogs, they make great sled animals. They are beautiful and intelligent but can also be darned destructive. This year, the outfitters are losing horses to wolf packs. Bears are also hard on horses.

The mother of one of our dogs was killed by the wolves just on the outskirts of town one winter. They left her tail and one tiny piece of hide—that's all. Her six pups were left unharmed.

I look upon the wolf with mixed emotions—I hate to see them chased and shot down by snow machine driving demons. I don't worry much about them being trapped because they are seldom stupid enough to walk into one. They have been declared big game this year; the trophy hunters will be after them. I hate to see the mauled remains of a wolf killed horse, but I'd hate to never again hear the beautiful voice of a wolf howling at night.

Wanted! A Northern Word

The other day, I was listening to a group of revelers talking about the great time they'd had at a recent Atlin dance. The discussion soon came around to colorful descriptions of varying stages of intoxication. This was done in humorous and descriptive prose. But later, it occurred to me that never once had a certain word entered the conversation, a word that some years ago was commonly used and perfectly acceptable at any social level. Its total absence from present day Canadian suggests it has, for some reason, been banned. Although it may be censored from this article, I'll put it down anyway because I think you should remember it and lament its loss.

The Word is D-R-U-N-K

Once this short and serviceable word was all that was needed to explain a state of being that is—ah—sort of common in these parts. And, although no one gets DRUNK anymore, they certainly do get some 554 other ways that all tally up to the same old thing.

Drunkenness now falls under a vast array of headings. It is one obsolete word that has been replaced by dozens and dozens of others. For instance, if you are kitchen-oriented, you can take your choice of getting STEWED, PICKLED, CROCKED, PIE-EYED, CORNED, FRIED, or POTTED.

Builders may become PLASTERED, STONED, or BLASTED. A service station operator might get GASSED, TANKED, or HOSED. An ecologist could possibly get POLLUTED but probably he would rather not. A trucker can get LOADED or JACK-KNIFED. See what I mean? Everything but D-R-U-N-K. People who are uptight might get TIGHT to relieve their uptightness but help is only temporary. Women who are over seventy get TIPSY only. That must have been permissible in their day and they haven't learned any of the other 553 ways to be.

Police shun the word DRUNK and all its derivatives but once they were sprinkled liberally across the blotter. Remember when people were arrested for DRUNKEN driving? Now it's IMPAIRED driving that lands you in the clink. Police used to give offenders a DRUNK-o-meter test. No more. It's the same old balloon with a new name, the breathalyzer.

The north is renowned for its accomplished drinkers and voluminous capacities. But, strangely, nowhere in the lengthy list of words describing (you should pardon the expression) DRUNKenesss is there one with a northern essence. If Whitehorse can have Yukon Hooch, then Atlin should have an exclusive word for what it does to you. We asked our readers for suggestions and the results were clever and imaginative. The famous northern weather provided several terms — ZEROED (or worse SUB-ZEROED), SNOWED, CRUSTED, FROSTED, ICE FOGGED, and FROST HEAVED. A trapper could find himself TANNED, SKINNED, FLAT-TRAPPED, SNARED, STRETCHED, or even CONNI-BEARED (apologies to Frank). A sawmill operator might get PLANNED, PLANKED, PEALED, FINISHED, or ROUGH-CUT, poor guy. A dog musher has a choice of getting GEED or HAWED in his dogged pursuit of liquor. The great mining industry provided some of the best descriptive terms. How would you like to spend New Year's Eve getting somewhat SLUICED, PANNED, STAKED, DRIFTED, or CLAIMED.

Perhaps you can send us your ideas. And remember, since it is no longer proper to get DRUNK, do something northern instead.

Your new dog sounds like a real pal. We have added one pup to our pack. He is black, friendly and smart but certainly no thing of beauty. But beauty and brains have little bearing on one another anyway. I have hopes he will be a lead dog for our team.

Of Porcupines and Dogs

Someone said they thought this was the Year of the Peacock for the Chinese but for the dog owners of Atlin, it is surely the Year of the Porcupine. It's with a sinking heart we hear someone say brightly, "I saw 67 porcupines on the road between here and Jake's Corner today." The porkies range abundant this summer and if there are two things that absolutely curdle when mixed together, it is porcupines and dogs.

A porcupine exudes a come-hither charm no canine can resist. But like a devil woman, it will leave an ardent pursuer coldly and painfully rejected—a little bit sadder but not necessarily a little wiser.

Sometimes a vindictive dog, incensed by the humiliating abuse handed him by a porky, becomes obsessed with revenge and spends a lifetime venting his ire on every porcupine he meets. We once had a dog who became porcupine addicted. He was a great brown mutt, flop-eared and gentle. He was half husky, half wet and smelly, and mostly lovable and stupid. He liked all cats and kids but learned to abhor all porkies. So tremendous was his obsession that he spent the hours in his kennel plotting the locations of every porcupine on the mountain behind our house. When the kennel door was opened, he could sprint out, find a porky, and be back at the kitchen door all hang-dog and quill-filled in exactly three minutes and eighteen seconds. He was such a continual patient at the veterinarian clinic we were given a special rate. The first dequilling each month cost $7.00. After that, they were on the house. The quill bill was paid regularly right along with the light and oil bills.

When you have a porcupine-addicted dog, you frequently find yourself listening to involved formulas for the easy extraction of quills eagerly offered by sympathetic friends, old timers, and liars. We have analyzed them all and tried many. Not a damned one worked.

One guy told how he jammed his arm down the throat of a two-hundred-pound quill-crazed dog as it reared up to devour him and pulled quills from its stomach all the way up. I suppose he could have performed an appendectomy at the same time if the dog had needed one.

Someone else suggested using ether to subdue the dog. So once when faced with three quill-skewered dogs, I managed to hustle some illegal ether and thought my problem was solved. Starting with a wee little dog named Sam, I advanced with a cotton wad reeking ether. "All you do is hold it to their nose until he goes to sleep," was the recipe. Sam and I sparred for a full hour. Sam was doing fine but I was about to embark on a trip from the ether. That was when I found out no dog with his tender nose full of quills is going to let anyone near that nose with anything if he can help it.

Also exploded were the theories about putting vinegar on the quills to soften them or cutting off their ends to let the air out. What air? If you can do all that first, the dog is dead! Brute force, a pair of pliers, and the guts to face the dripping fangs of your quill-maddened Rover are the only answer—unless there is a veterinarian handy. Unfortunately for Atlinite's, the nearest one lives in another country.

One day we gave one of our dogs three sleeping pills before the dequilling ordeal. After an hour, it appeared the pills weren't going to work. So, the dog was compressed tightly to the floor by the weight of two large men and the quills were pulled. Afterward she doled out a dirty look and stalked out of the house. Then at dinner time, four hours later she reeled back in like a drunk on a three-day jag. She stumbled over the cat, stepped in the water dish, and ran into a chair. All four skinny legs were braided. Finally, she fell on her back under the table with her paws crossed on her chest and began snoring. A lifted lid revealed a glassy eyeball. We could have skinned her then and she would never have shown a tooth.

I don't know anything nice to say about the combination of dogs and porcupines, but I do know a lot of other things. For instance, an older dog will lead a pup to a porcupine and stand back laughing and scratching while the innocent pup rushes up and gets a painful swat in the face. I know it takes two strong men and a woman (if the third guy has a weak stomach and goes home) to hold down a hundred-pound screaming, bleeding Malamute and pull his quills.

The average Canadian porcupine has thirty thousand quills. Someone once clocked a quill and found it can travel up to two inches a day through a dog. The encyclopedia talks a lot about porcupine's teeth but they aren't on the end that gives dogs all the trouble.

For some reason the compartment of the canine brain labeled "porcupine" is always void. Just when you figure your favorite dog has learned to steer clear of porcupines, he will go out and get a worse snoot full of quills than he ever had before. About the only thing Atlin dog owners can hope for is that next year the Chinese get all the porcupines and we get the peacocks instead.

My husband bought lots of nice pelts from trappers this winter as well as trapping his own fur. Because there were lots of rabbits, there were also lots of their predators: fox, lynx, wolf, coyote, etc. My shop is full and so is the back closet where I keep the pelts cool until I send them off for tanning.

The Indian River Monster

On July 11, a mysterious serpentine-like creature was sighted just off the beach of the mouth of Indian River, twenty miles north of Atlin. The sighting took place at approximately two thirty p.m. The day was bright and clear and the water calm.

The Simpsons were picnicking with their three children and a young friend of the family. Mrs. Simpson had left the party and wandered a short distance along the beach where she decided to sit in the sun and doze a bit. While so engaged, she was suddenly aroused by an unusual sound, "Unk! Unk!" The noise disturbed her but she didn't immediately open her eyes. Then the sound came again, "Unk! Unk!" more insistent this time. Now full alert, Mrs. Simpson turned her head toward the lake from where the disturbance came. What she saw astounded and thoroughly frightened her. She leapt to her feet. In the lake a scant fifteen feet away, was a black, shiny creature about twenty feet in length. It had three distinct heads in tandem at the front end and there were four undulating humps following along behind.

The sight was so grotesque and unexpected that Mrs. Simpson involuntarily shrieked in horror. At her outburst of terror, all three heads swiveled toward her in unison, fixing her with a malevolent stare and repeating the strange "Unk! Unk!"

With winged feet, Mrs. Simpson fled screaming along the beach to her family beseeching her husband to save her from the fiendish monster. Mr. Simpson stepped to the edge of the water and cast his steely gaze upon the ghastly beast. To his surprise, he saw it speedily change course and make its way to the opposite shore.

When the panic had subsided, the little group, with some apprehension, resumed fishing though they maintained a wary lookout over the menacing water.

Two hours later as the picnickers were gathering their things in preparation for their return to Atlin, Mr. Simpson shouted and pointed toward the lake. With a ringing voice, he announced the return of the strange manifestation. The group stood breathless and poised for flight. Then to their amazement, the creature separated into seven individual bodies right before their gaze. In the murky half-light of evening, it was impossible to ascertain exactly what had occurred. For some time, the creature cavorted near the shoreline. Sometimes there were seven things visible, sometimes five or three, but always at least one was in sight. Perplexed and uneasy, the picnickers left the disturbing scene and drove slowly home.

The next day in intense consultation with experts in the field of aquatic analogies, it was finally determined unquestionably that the Simpson party had seen the rare and unusual elusive Australoatlinus, commonly called "Attie." It is believed the only other sighting of "Attie" occurred some years ago in the same vicinity. At that time, Mr. Tom Coleman, Esquire, of Atlin, saw five "Atties" undulating along the highway during the snowy winter season.

For those of you not familiar with Australoatlinus, it has yet another name, Lutra Canadensis. In other words, it is the Otter. The common land otter is about four feet long at maturity and often several otters travel in single file on either land or in the water. The Indian River Monster was a party of seven otters.

If you enjoyed this episode in the lives and adventures of the Simpsons, don't miss next week's issue of the *Atlin News Miner* where you can read the next installment of Mrs. Simpson, Mrs. Simpson.

Unk! Unk!

I am sorry to find your service is so poor. This is not the first time I have waited several weeks for items advertised in your catalog. It seems incredible you include items which you are obviously not prepared to sell. You should realize that your northern customers have a very short summer season and would like items of summer clothing sent at once.

House Husband Wanted

The five members of Atlin Ladies Co-Op wish to share a house husband. No previous experience required. However, applicant must be amiable, charming, tall, and have clean finger nails. He should also be bi-lingual: Canadian and American. He must be resourceful, ingenious, and patient. He should have a basic knowledge of child psychology, diapers, and runny noses. Although cooking meals is not required by all co-op members, those wishing him to cook will expect well-prepared nutritious meals that are attractively served and low in calories.

Applicants must be able to do bookkeeping, although not definitely required, a degree in economics and business administration will be given special attention.

House husband applicant should furnish his own calculator, cookbooks, aprons, and aspirin. Candlelight and wine will be provided by co-op members as required. Applicant will at times be required to carry on normal household duties such as laundering, cooking, cleaning, and scrubbing grubby kids in residence where there is no running water (or often no water at all if the truck breaks down), no indoor plumbing or aides such as dishwashers, bathtubs, automatic washing machines, or dryers.

Applicant must be able to operate all regular electrical appliances such as vacuum cleaners, blenders, eight-track tape decks, and diesel generators. He should have a good working knowledge of chainsaws, bicycle pumps, tinker toys, and Frisbees.

House husband duties will cover the period between 8am to 8pm daily as well as the hours from 10pm to midnight for one co-op member who prefers companionship only.

Fringe benefits will be given at the discretion of each of co-op member. Salary will be worked out on a running scale and awarded according to efficiency and amount of work accomplished.

All interested men may send applications to Atlin Ladies House Husband Co-op, Atlin, BC You will be informed of place and time of your interview within a week.

Well, I've rambled on long enough about our northern village. I always do when I have a chance. Most people hardly realize there are still frontier towns like this. I see the excitement of the tourists each summer when they discover Atlin with its gold-camp look still predominant.

Atlin Househusbands Co-operative

Due to the overwhelming response for membership applications to the Atlin Househusbands Co-op, and a disappointing lack of applicants for the househusbands position, we have decided to change the requirements, thus making it possible for more interested men to apply. The demand for househusbands has definitely increased over the last month.

First of all, since there are few applicants that can fix frisbees, this requirement has been deleted.

Degrees in child psychology, economics and business administration will be waived in lieu of on-the-job training.

Calculators, cookbooks, aprons and aspirin will now be provided by the Co-op members.

Normal household duties such as laundering, cooking, cleaning, and scrubbing dirty kids will be compensated for by additional fringe benefits.

Hours of duties have been changed to noon to 4:30 p.m daily. (4:30 p.m. is happy hour time which will of course be attended by Co-op members and househusbands.)

Applicant will no longer be required to speak American, or for that matter Canadian—just body language.

The hours from 10 p.m. until midnight, for the co-op member who prefers companionship only, have been reduced, after heated negotiations, from 10 p.m. to 11:30 p.m.

Fringe benefits have been substantially increased as has the salary. Both will be worked out on a sliding scale and awarded as originally planned, according to efficiency and amount of work accomplished.

A relisting of requirements for househusband applicant is as follows.

1) Must be male
2) That's it

All interested men may send applications to the Atlin Ladies Househusbands Co-Op, Atlin BC Just think—you may be the person we are seeking! Looking forward to hearing from you.

Edie Crum shops for gifts while Diane Smith prepares to pack them. For the second year, Atlin residents have enjoyed Christmas shopping for "Made in Atlin" gifts. Diane Smith's Discovery Shop, which was Atlin's first arts and crafts shop set up displays of jewelry, leather craft, wood carvings, knitting of home-spun yarns, paintings, etc. to fill the old Court Room. Participating in the event were Bob Fassel—wood carvings, Jan Harvey—items from "The Gallery," Claudia Lombardi—hand knittings, Sue Beadman—machine knit items, Alma Fassel—gingerbread houses, Peggy Milius—oil paintings, and of course, leather work, gold jewelry, etc. by Diane Smith.

Arts and Crafts and Sales

A certain industry has come into the limelight of late. It has been around ever since man first discovered what his fingers were for, but it used to be seen mostly at church bazaars and school fund raisers. This is the fast-growing crafts industry.

Last winter, I received a government questionnaire concerning crafts and my part in the scene. I knew there was something big happening. Arts and crafts had to be making a noticeable wave on the national sea of economics for Ottawa to be so interested. Perhaps the government is going to allot funds for retired or indigent artists or maybe arrange UIC for the unemployed craftsman. More likely, the government smells money and wants a piece of the action. This I view with a wary eye.

The return to handcrafts started in the murky days of counter culture revolutions when establishment was a bad word and living organically was in. When the rebels shoved off for the bush to make a stab at the old-time way of life, they soon found out the barter system was not about to be revived and horse trading could only account for a part of their needs. They had to do something for money. So they made things and sold them. Some of the things created in those back woodsy retreats were beautifully done. Old ideas were given new twists and produced one by one with care and purity.

At about the same time, the erstwhile consumer was rankling at the cookie cut-out perfect stuff that rolled in endless files from assembly lines. Plastics, synthetics, and chrome, once so fascinating, had become dullsville. The buyer yearned for handmade products–those neat things that had flaws and finger marks to show they had indeed been touched by human hands.

Ironically while the straights viewed the kids in jeans and tousled mops with raised eyebrows, they clamored to buy their wares. It was soon clearly shown that, given a chance, the average consumer was a person of discriminate taste.

The truth of the crafts revival was proven in November at the Spruce Bog County Fair held in Whitehorse by the Yukon Crafts Society. Some fifty craftsmen and artists displayed and sold their work in the elementary school gymnasium while determined Christmas shoppers packed the place until breathing became a chore. I noted that craftsmen and buyers looked very much alike. Gone is the old image of the down at the heels floaty sort of craftsman. Serious craftsmen are just people who work at their arts because they can make money doing something for which they have a talent and which they enjoy.

The quality of work at the Spruce Bog was good. Variety was great. There was everything from photography and oil paintings to rag dolls, not to mention Christmas cakes stuffed with fruit and nuts and loaded with rum.

The work of twelve Atlin artists and craftsmen was on sale in Whitehorse. Most of these exhibitors were ready within a week to put on the Atlin Arts Annual Christmas Crafts sale here. Several new people joined the Atlin group this year bringing more choice to local buyers.

Atlin is now well known in this northern area for its fine craft work and art. The number of Atlin people who make all or a part of their living working artistically has grown steadily during the last few years. The inspiring mountain setting of Atlin probably has been a strong influence on craftsmen who have moved here but others have turned to the crafts after long residence discovering inner talents long neglected or little known. More people involved in the crafts means a better chance for exchanging ideas or just egging each other on. It seems a fair prediction that Atlin arts and crafts will continue to spread their fame far beyond the fringes of this wilderness.

You may use the cabin free of charge while you are getting settled and until you find a better place. You can do whatever you want to brighten or fix it up or nothing if you would rather save time and effort for something more important. You will need a stove. There is a "rustic" table and cupboards with doors. That's about all. I think the roof is tight so the cabin might be a good place to store your gear if nothing else. If this will help you feel free—we'd be glad to have you.

The Atlin Security Blanket

Everyone has heard of the physiological security blanket. It is the end result of a behavior motivation which leads to saving something, be it money or stale sourdoughs, thus creating a shield against unexpected needs or threatening events. For an infant, a soggy thumb is all that is needed to ward off demons conjured up in his baby brain. But with adults, this activity can take off in unexpected directions and Atlin adults in particular wrap themselves in intricately woven security blankets. The semi-isolation, long dark days, and severe cold of winter has given a whole new twist to the old string and tinfoil saving pattern.

For the cheechakos, still casting about for your own best security blanket, here are some ideas gathered from Atlin old timers. Maybe they will help you find an answer to the apprehensions and pesky little inconveniences of your first northern winter.

Books are one of the world's best security blankets because reading is an effective escape mechanism and this is what we most often need during an Atlin winter. Reading a good book can project you happily into some other world while you sit in your living room where the temperature is 36 degrees knowing full well Harvey Rossiter has 28 other deliveries to make before he can fill your oil barrels.

A good book will relieve the discomfort of waiting for the septic tank to be emptied. Sometimes this takes until June. You might need three or four books when you have three teaspoons of water in the whole house, there are 18 dinner guests arriving in just 35 minutes, the budgie is dying of thirst and Ron Bowdin and his water truck have vanished from the face of the earth. Best of all, however, a book will dispel the dismal feeling discovering there is no toilet paper or peanut butter at either The Trading Post or Edie's Store until next Wednesday.

Security precautions must be taken against the possibility of winter idleness which leads directly to advanced cabin fever. Here an enormous store of "work-needing-to-be-done" is all you have to have. For instance, about thirteen broken chainsaws and three non-running snow machines with lots of missing parts are excellent. A large basket containing 85 balls of yarn and a half-finished hand knit jumpsuit for a 290-pound man is great as is a 45-gallon drum filled with miscellaneous nuts, bolts, screws, nails, and copper fittings which need to be sorted.

Our pioneer backgrounds decree we must always be

working. Unless one is totally devoid of conscience, he must be doing something that falls somewhere under the heading of work at any given time in the day. The woman who bakes has at her finger tips the best security blanket in the entire non-idleness' department. As long as she has bread doing something in the kitchen, she has an airtight alibi for sitting around the Trappers Coffee House drinking tea or spending three hours at the magazine rack at the General Store. When the bread is doing something at home, she can while away guilt-free hours talking about all the work she has been doing to some other gal who also has bread going for her.

Having a lot of dogs is a legendary sort of security which harkens from the old story of cuddling up with mutts on cold nights: hence the terms "one dog night" or the cooler "two dog night." Even realizing fully the dog blanket business is lore, just the knowledge there are eight woolly smelly dogs out there somewhere ready and waiting in case the electric blanket fails beats some of the most carefully contrived schemes.

Being alone can be a dangerous winter situation but is easily remedied. You should keep on hand a very large selection of the following items: copper fittings, nuts, bolts, and screws, oil, water, recipes for making bread, peanut butter, and toilet paper. These are the things people most often have to borrow in Atlin and if everyone knows that you always have all of them, they will be beating a path to your door and you will never know that awful feeling that no one loves you. And it will be spring before you know it.

I spent nearly all my spare time, with the help of my friend Peggy, remodeling an old house into which we have now moved. It was hectic but we managed and I'm quite proud of our carpentry skills. Our next project on the priority list is to remodel an old cabin across the street from where we now live. It will then be The Discovery Shop. With warmer weather and a bit of experience behind us we are looking forward to this job but I do have to hurry. Already visitors from outside are here looking for gift items.

People and a Small Northern Town

Walk along an Atlin street on a soft summer night. Across your way, spears of light from curtained windows make warm, inviting patterns on the gravel. Behind darkened doorways, sounds of a town alive and growing, trickle into the night—a muffled laugh, a child's sleepy cry, garbled words, the noises of families deep in the business of an evening. They are comfortable and secure sounds.

Two young people representing opposite ends of the continent meet in a small northern town. Something

86

clicks between them; shreds of loneliness fall away and they decide to join forces. A new life begins for them and adds to the general din of progress.

Atlin is a town experiencing a rebirth. In a few short years it has thrown off the robes of a ghost town—squashed that title with little ceremony. Derelict buildings have been painted and occupied, vacant lots have sprouted handsome log structures, the "city" limits have been pushed back. These things have occurred because of people, and people are what small northern towns are all about. It isn't an easy task bringing a town back. People being what they are, complex and unpredictable creatures, a certain percentage are lost in the effort. Sadness and despair may end a sojourn, and partners split to travel separate ways wondering where things went wrong that once seemed so right. Others would never fit in and eventually they drift on.

People thrown together in semi-isolation and hounded by hostile weather are sometimes deprived of the ability to think objectively. Problems loom too close and too large. Irritations fester. All around is wilderness, sometimes friendly, often oppressive and confining, making it impossible to back away and see things for their actual worth. Gossip can run rampant and malignant. Tempers flare and prejudices are cultivated.

The wounds inflicted by a small town can be deep and bitterly painful. But, by the same token, the good times working together for an important common goal are gratifying. Honors given are cherished because they are warm and personal.

A tough tenacious fiber is evident in the makeup of the people willing to put up with the rough climate, cabin fever, and small-town discontent to live in the north. Inconveniences and community gripes are endured, not always graciously, but endured nevertheless for the compensations on the credit side of the ledger. The feeling of being an individual, one unique human being, is probably the most important prize granted to a northerner. He counts. Good or bad, his influence is felt and adds an important ingredient to the mixture that comprises his small northern town. In Atlin, the recipe seems a success. The town is alive and thriving in northern British Columbia. It's the people that made it happen.

Brad and I went grouse hunting a couple weekends but found ourselves exploring instead. We drove my battered car all the way to Adnac Mine one Sunday—over roads that resembled goat trails way up above timberline. We had a small blizzard and lots of wind, but it was really exciting. We saw some ptarmigan—no grouse—and aside from stopping down by Surprise Lake for a little target practice, we didn't shoot a thing. The next time we ended up at Atlin Silver Mine and Brad did get one grouse out of the three we flushed. Apparently, the hot grouse hunting was up Wright Creek this year.

The Curse of the Engineer Mine

Engineer Mine lies bleak and still on the ragged shore of Tagish Lake. Gray gaping buildings look across lonely waters where once stern wheelers plied on regular schedules and the ring of mining filled the air. Engineer played an important part in the history of the Atlin Mining District but it was an antagonizing, on and off again mine right from the start. Extremely rich veins produced gloriously then pinched off and disappeared to the consternation of the men working there. It was inconsistent in its riches and those who really struck it rich at Engineer were few.

Some years after the first Engineer claims were recorded, a strangely mysterious man, one Captain James Alexander, entered the picture. His dealings at the start brought down upon the mine a curse that plagued those concerned with it with death and disaster for many dark years.

Harper Reed, Indian Agent, miner and noted pioneer of Stikine and Atlin regions became involved with the Engineer Mine upon the demise of Captain Alexander. He knew the black story of Engineer and its curse and in the later years of his life he wrote a brief history telling of the strange events surrounding it.

The following is Reed's story into which I have injected information from old Minister of Mines reports. There are some discrepancies in Reed's report but much of his information may have been gleaned from what was common local knowledge of his day. A strange bit of history that has been all but forgotten.

During the construction of the White Pass and Yukon Railroad at the turn of the century, several of the engineers from the job, intrigued with prospecting, ventured into the Tagish Lake area in search of gold. They found it on the Eastern shore of the lake—small stringers of quarts carrying free gold visible to the eye. They staked claims and formed the Engineer Mining Company at Skagway. When the railroad was completed, these men dispersed to the states, but the next summer the chief engineer returned with a small crew of men to do assessment work.

He went to Atlin to record the work they had accomplished and here fate led him to Captain Alexander seeking information on how to do his recording.

Alexander had reached a low point financially and

he skillfully laid a trap for the young greenhorn. He persuaded him to include false expenses in his report then later had friends on the police force confront him with sworn information about this falsifying. He was thrown into jail. Alexander then stepped forward and offered his aid telling the young engineer he could get him out of trouble if he would withdraw the recording of his claims and leave the country. Glad to be freed from his humiliating situation, the engineer complied at once.

A few months after duping the engineer, Alexander staked the claims on Tagish Lake when they were thrown open again. His partner was a Swede named Olson. Soon after recording the claims, Alexander either forced or bought out Olson for the meager sum of $300.00.

One of the Engineer Mining Company syndicate members, a man named Brown, heard of Alexander's underhanded dealings and confronted him. He told Alexander that if he persisted in recording and working the claims, nothing but evil would result. He formally and solemnly put a curse on the property saying that death and disaster would be the lot of Alexander or anyone having anything to do with Engineer Mine.

Alexander was an Australian, a soldier of fortune. He was known to be a man of great physical strength and he was a heavy drinker. He possessed some knowledge of mining and he chose to ignore Brown's curse.

Going ahead with his plans, Alexander staked more claims. The two-stamp mill started by the engineers were completed and a few tons of high-grade ore treated by amalgamation. The mine apparently produced some tonnage of spectacular ore but Alexander was secretive about it and would allow no one to inspect the property except an occasional engineer hired by him.

In 1912, he acquired his partners' interests and continued prospecting on a more systematic basis finding formerly unknown bodies of such high values of free gold that the stamp mill produced bullion worth $26,000 in 1913 and $20,000 in 1914.

Although Harper Reed reported Alexander a secretive loner working the mine only during the summer, the Ministry of Mines report records that he had six to twenty-eight men employed throughout most of 1915. Some concentrates were shipped to the smelter and a "snug cleanup" in bullion recovered.

However, most men found the captain an odd sort given to long drinking bouts. His one real contribution to the Northern society was Polly, the parrot. He brought her into the country around 1917 and she was no youngster then.

Alexander mined Engineer and traveled out to Vancouver each year to blow the gold he gained in painting the town a vivid, livid scarlet. His mining and winning continued until 1918.

In that year, a young engineer named George Randolph was sent by the Mining Corporation of Canada to look over the properties in BC with an eye to options. Later, the manager of Mining Corp., Charles Watson, along with C.L. Clabon, one of the principals, were in BC looking over the options Randolph had already obtained. Watson received a wire while they were in Revelstoke to proceed at once to the Engineer Mine. He and Randolph left and a few days later received word Clabon had fallen over a cliff at the Revelstoke Mine and was instantly killed. The curse of Brown was beginning to work.

In the meantime, a New York engineer, Wayne Darlington had succeeded where others had failed. He obtained an option from Alexander on the Engineer Mine, and in turn passed it on to the Mining Corp. In Vancouver, Alexander met with Verrall, an engineer representing Darlington,

Watson and Randolph, and together with Alexander's wife, they sailed north.

After an inspection of the properties on Tagish Lake, they all returned to Skagway to catch the last ship south for the winter. This time disaster struck with a vengeance. The Canadian Pacific Railway steamship, Princes Sophia, ran aground on Vanderbilt Reef just north of Juneau. The ship hung there for nearly two days while the skipper refused to disembark his passengers to rescue boats thinking the next high tide would free the grounded vessel. Instead, a wild storm struck in the night and the Sophia ripped open and sank while rescue craft hovered in the lee of a nearby island. Alexander, his wife, Verrall, Randolph, and Watson counted among the 357 people who drowned in that tragic wreck.

Following the disaster, Harper Reed was sent to Vancouver by the Mining Corp. and there learned more of Alexander's habits and unusual business affairs. He discovered there was a silent partner in Philadelphia, one Alan Smith who by then was in Vancouver. Smith claimed there existed an agreement drawn up between him and the captain, stating that should one die, the other would receive his share of the Engineer Mine.

A messenger was dispatched from Carcross to Engineer Mine to find the document at the mine office. He traveled over the lake ice but on his return, he broke through and drowned. Later his back pack was found near the hole in the ice and its contents revealed that the woman who had posed as Mrs. Alexander was not his wife at all.

His legal wife and sixteen-year-old daughter lived in England. The real Mrs. Alexander started litigations but within a year, she also died and the daughter was left to carry on the suit. All this time, the mine lay idle.

In 1923, five years after Alexander's death, the Mining Corp received word from Alan Smith that litigations were settled and he was now able to deal. A man was sent to meet with him, but Smith was also a heavy drinker and nothing could be accomplished. Shortly afterward, Alan Smith committed suicide.

In a 1930, C.V. Bob, a New York financier, undertook to operate Engineer Mine. He hired an engineer, a newly wed, who was to proceed with his bride to Canada. Again, the curse struck. The young engineer slipped under the moving train he was boarding and was killed. Then Mr. Bob came under the scrutiny of the American authorities for his stock market dealings and was hustled off to jail.

In 1934, the Mining Corporation of Canada was in the scene again. The assets of Engineer Mine were sold to them at a sheriff's sale for $25,000. The next year, the director of the Corporation died, followed in death the next year by yet another director.

In 1936, a John E. Hammel arranged an option on the property with the Mining Corp. He fired an engineer who had previous experience at the mine but was then in the Philippines. Before the engineer could leave for Canada, he fell down a shaft in the Philippine mine and was killed.

Here at last the curse seemed to have run its evil course and ceased at last to plague the ill-fated mine. Others have mined there since without tragic results but also without much financial success.

Engineer Mine has not been forgotten, abandoned though it may appear. The property has been held continuously throughout the years and it will probably always have a magnetic draw for gold seekers.

As for Polly, the Captain left her in the care of the Caribou Hotel at Carcross the winter he made his last voyage on the Sophia, and there Polly remained until she died at the age of about 126 last winter. Obviously, the Engineer curse did not include her.

Well, with my husband gone except for short trips home every couple months. Young son and I had to brave the wily ways of winter alone. Every time it got to minus fifty or more, the furnace would stop operating, usually at night. The sewer line to the tank froze up in November and the waterline from the holding tank in September. Normally, we have water delivered to a hundred-gallon storage tank downstairs. Then we pump it up to the kitchen sink and toilet. We have a septic tank to handle the toilet and gray water when it's not frozen solid.

As you know, we live in the old historic court house. The living quarters are up two flights of stairs under the hip roof. As the lower floor is fifty by fifty with eighteen-foot ceilings, we do not and could not afford to heat it. All water and waste has to come up and down two long flights of stairs in five-gallon buckets. Thank goodness for the outhouse. I had the waterman fill two thirty-gallon plastic garbage cans by the front door downstairs as his hose will not reach all the way upstairs. In the kitchen, we have a forty-five-gallon barrel. On water day, Brad and I bail water and haul it up to the kitchen until the barrel is full. The remainder freezes in the can and then we drag and pull it up to thaw out later. The joys of remote living.

Freeze Up

The leaves are yellow. The blue-red blaze of the fireweed has gone out. Left in the dying embers are little wisps of smoky seed things floating on crisp air. Fall is here and if this be true, close behind it blowing a frigid, warning breath down the necks of Atlinites is Freeze Up!

Freeze Up! The very words can strike terror into any heart. Freeze Up! The man who has yet to install a septic tank is stopped dead in his path by the sight of morning frost on a neighbor's roof. Freeze Up! The house painter throws down his fishing rod and runs desperately with bucket and ladder knowing full well the latex will freeze on his brush before the job is done.

Freeze Up! The old lead ball forms in the stomach pit of the summer idler and jolts him rudely from his warm-weather lethargy. As if for the first time, he sees the carefully compiled list of summer projects tacked to the kitchen door. All season it waved unnoticed as he steamed with cold beers and picnic basket.

Now as though emblazoned with neon, it taunts him. "Hey, Dad," it sneers, "you have 23 major projects to complete before Freeze Up. Would you like to start with Item No. 1. Cut 18 cords of wood. Or would you prefer Item No. 5. Install backyard fence. That one only requires the digging of 27 post holes."

With a forced smile of nonchalance, Mr. Summer Fun and Games scuttles out of town to the nearest burn with his chainsaw clutched in a clammy hand. He passes a neighbor casually starting to put in a concrete foundation for a new garage. He detects the frantic "I'll never make it" look in the man's eyes and tries to glean some small bit of comfort from another's misery.

About town, the pace quickens. Coffee klatches become short and a leisurely chat with the guy next door may end abruptly when his eyes wander to his roof and he remembers there is a large leaky place to be patched up there before the snow flies. There is a regular conversation in the berry patch as flying fingers fill yawning lard pails. Item No. 6. Make 48 jars of jam and freeze 45 pounds of berries.

Catalogs are worn to crumpled rags as pages are

thumbed in desperate search for warm caps and mitts even though hope is dim, they will still be available. Why didn't you order everything last July when the winter catalogue first arrived? But back in those balmy, palmy days, who could consider things like ice and snow and . . . Freeze Up!

Unless life in Atlin has changed, this fall will be like all the falls before it. The zero-hour race will prevail until about October 18. Then one morning the ground will be very white and very stiff, but out in the new garage, the freezer will be humming merrily full of moose meat and berries. Eighteen cords of wood will be stacked by the kitchen door which is no longer graced with that menacing decree of blood-red letters. Summer clothes will be stored and dresser drawers stuffed with woolly long johns and socks because Arthur and Nancy down at the General Store remembered to order enough for everyone. Two sides of the house won't be painted, but down under that frozen ground the new septic tank will be busy doing its thing.

The coffee klatches again grow long and stimulating as conversation turns easily to winter things. The frantic eyes have a new "we did it again smirk" about them, and the once dreaded words Freeze Up! bring to mind only things like snowmobiling, cross-country skiing, and "Anyone for dog mushing and curling?"

Tom Kirkwood, Editor of the *Atlin News Miner*

The Birth of the Modern *Atlin News Miner*

One man had a dream and through hard work and a relentless persistence, his dream became an improbable and glorious reality.

That man's name was Tom Kirkwood and his dream was to be a newspaper man. Tom may have let it slip on an occasion that his newspaper endeavor was a thinly veiled attempt to bolster Atlin's ever struggling economy but either way on June 1, 1972, the modern *Atlin News Miner* released its inaugural edition and became the first newspaper to service Atlin in many decades bringing Tom's dream/scheme to fulfillment.

Tom was the editor and chief and his wife Vera was everything else. Tom was able to finagle a deal with the then owners of the Whitehorse Star Newspaper, Bob and Rusty Erlam who subsidized most of the cost of printing and distribution.

The modern *Atlin News Miner* was an instant success in Atlin as well as Whitehorse. Although the town population was around 250 at the time of the first publication, subscriptions quickly neared 400 with subscribers across Canada and the United States and even a few in Europe. It seemed anyone with even the slightest ties to Atlin was hungry for the local news.

Tom reported on all community events and took copious photos which appeared in the paper. Tom also wrote editorials and answered letters to the editor. Vera shared writing duties on a comings and goings around town column. She also had a long running recipe and cooking series as well as helping Tom with all the details that go into publishing a bimonthly newspaper.

Many residents contributed articles and updates. Every edition offered a RCMP and a Fish and Game report, a health update from the Red Cross outpost and news from the various clubs and organizations. The principal of the school reported on recent and upcoming events at Atlin's tiny school. Both churches offered congratulations and dates for weddings, baptisms, fundraisers, and activities. School children contributed poems, stories, and artwork. Every track meet and curling event, home or away, was reported in depth and all results were proudly recorded with pictures included.

Citizens offered recipes for their favorite wildlife dish or sent in an occasionally poem, cartoon, or random article pertaining to current events. There was no shortage of contributors and there were more than a few madcap stories of pounding away on the typewriter until the wee hours of the morning to make a deadline. It's not a stretch to say Tom and others risked their lives battling blizzards and horrible road conditions to get the current edition to the printer in Whitehorse on time.

The modern *Atlin News Miner* ran from 1972 until its last edition, October 17, 1978. Truly, it was a community effort in every sense. The modern *Atlin News Miner* was an example of how one person's dream with the help of their community can come to fruition no matter the struggle.

Unrealized at the time, the *Atlin News Miner* has become a great historic resource as it provides an encompassing study of a small community during a particular period of time.

Never doubt that a small group of thoughtful, committed citizens can change the world. Indeed, it is the only thing that ever has.   Margaret Mead

This is the last issue of the *Atlin News Miner*. Thank you to all those who have been a part of this publication. Particularly to Bob and Paul Erlam of the Whitehorse Star who have published and subsidized the *Atlin News Miner*.

The *Atlin News Miner* for the time being has come to another ending. The paper served Atlin from 1940 to 1943 when it could no longed make its way and ceased publication.

There are a number of reasons. The Whitehorse Star who publishes our paper went daily about a year ago. From that time on, it has become increasingly difficult to fit the *Atlin News Miner* into their busy schedule as they also print several other papers for Inuvik, Cassiar, the Native Brotherhood, and several others all of whom pay their way. Over the past six years, Atlin has had a newspaper because Bob and Paul have subsidized printing costs.

For Vera said it, it has become very time consuming. Each issue takes up five days to write it up, have it printed and mailed out. Without the help a good number of local people, it would indeed take a great more time.

To all those who have written articles for the *Atlin News Miner*, our most sincere thanks for being an integral part. To those who have assisted in the mailing, again our sincere thanks. To the businesses, particularly of Whitehorse who have used our advertising media—an appreciative thank you.

To the Whitehorse Star, Bob and Paul Erlam, we wish to extend our thanks for having given Atlin its own newspaper for the past six years.

Perhaps at some future date an opportunity may present itself so that the *Atlin News Miner* may once again be revived.

To our readers, a thank you for having put up with our sometime erratic publishing.

Diane Solie Smith

As a young girl, Diane was given Jack London's book, *White Fang*, by her father. It is hard to say if that book ignited a lifelong calling to the north, but it is certain she ended up there.

Born and raised in Washington state, her childhood was filled with fishing, hunting, skiing, and swimming. Little did she know then that she was preparing herself for her northern future.

While studying art at the University of Washington, she switched her major to engineering as she feared becoming another starving artist.

Immediately after graduation, she accepted a job as a civil engineer at the Bremerton Navy Shipyard where she would be involved in, among other projects, modifying and developing the new steam catapult system on Essex class aircraft carriers.

It was while working for the navy that she learned of a job opening with the Coast Guard in Juneau, Alaska. Within weeks, she was Juneau's newest resident. There she would marry and have a son. Diane soon grew tired of the hum-drum office life and although she had fallen in love with the north country and the people, she couldn't help thinking there was more.

In 1967, with a relatively new husband and even newer son, she moved to Atlin, British Columbia. In those days, there wasn't much thought put toward delineating borders between Alaska and Canada. The north was the north and that was that. The Canadian government seemed glad to have her and her family and four dogs and little fuss was made.

Diane knew when she first rounded the last bend in the road and saw Atlin Mountain and the beautiful body of water stretched out before it that she had found her new and forever home.

Although she often drew plans for Atlin's new buildings, her engineering degree would mostly collect dust. On the other hand, her artistic talent served her well in the ensuing years, and at times, was the only thing that kept food on the table.

Diane opened a gift shop and sold her own wares as well as offering space for other artists and craftsmen. At the same time, she and her husband put together a small museum. Diane readily turned over the museum to the newly-formed Atlin Historical Society. She kept active in the museum and the Society for the rest of her life.

Diane went on to write the quintessential history, *Atlin: The Story of British Columbia's Last Gold Rush* with writing partner Christine Frances Dickinson. Diane also wrote several other historical publications that are still sold at the museum.

Diane lived the rest of her life in Atlin where she was, among other things, a business owner, a historian, a prolific artist well versed in multiple mediums. She was a gifted archivist who transcribed many gold rush journals and diaries to preserve important local history.

Diane was a dog musher, a carpenter, a trapper, an author, a columnist, a single mother, and a champion of all things Atlin. She passed away in 2003 and was laid to rest on a hillside blanketed with wildflowers overlooking the land and town she loved.

Books by Diane Solie Smith

The Way It Used To Be
Diane Solie Smith, Bradford D. Smith, Editor
Fathom Publishing (2024)

The Legend of Lillian Alling:
  The Woman Who Walked to Russia
Diane Solie Smith
Atlin Historical Society (2001)

A Guide to Atlin's Historic Buildings
Diane Solie Smith
Atlin Historical Society (2003)

Atlin: The Story of British Columbia's Last Gold Rush
Christine Frances Dickinson and Diane Solie Smith
Atlin Historical Society (1995)

Atlin Where Everyone Knows Your Dog's Name
Bradford D. Smith and Diane Solie Smith
Fathom Publishing (2021)

Available from Atlin Historical Society
https://www.atlinhistoricalsociety.ca

www.ingramcontent.com/pod-product-compliance
Lightning Source LLC
Chambersburg PA
CBHW070959120626
46546CB00004B/1699